D0059231

How to

Be a Couple

and

Still Be Free

Third Edition

YOLO COUNTY LIBRARY
226 BUCKEYE STREET
WOODLAND, CA 95695-2600

How to

Be a Couple

and

Still Be Free

Third Edition

By
Tina Tessina, Ph.D.
Riley K. Smith, M.A.

NEW PAGE BOOKS
A division of The Career Press, Inc.
Franklin Lakes, NJ

Copyright © 2002 by Tina Tessina and Riley K. Smith

All rights reserved under the Pan-American and International Copyright Conventions. This book may not be reproduced, in whole or in part, in any form or by any means electronic or mechanical, including photocopying, recording, or by any information storage and retrieval system now known or hereafter invented, without written permission from the publisher, The Career Press.

HOW TO BE A COUPLE AND STILL BE FREE 3RD EDITION
Edited and Typeset by Kristen Mohn
Cover design by Design Concept
Printed in the U.S.A. by Book-mart Press

To order this title, please call toll-free 1-800-CAREER-1 (NJ and Canada: 201-848-0310) to order using VISA or MasterCard, or for further information on books from Career Press.

The Career Press, Inc., 3 Tice Road, PO Box 687,
Franklin Lakes, NJ 07417
www.careerpress.com
www.newpagebooks.com

Library of Congress Cataloging-in-Publication Data
Tessina, Tina B.
   How to be a couple and still be free / by Tina Tessina and Riley K. Smith.—3rd ed.
     p. cm.
   Includes index.
   ISBN 1-56414-549-2 (pbk.)
   1. Couples. 2. Interpersonal relations. 3. Intimacy (Psychology) 4. Problem solving. 5. Self-actualization (Psychology) I. Smith, Riley K. II. Title.

HQ801 .T368 2002
306.7—dc21

                                      2001052168

*We dedicate this book
to Amanda Halley Bialack, age 15,
who is rapidly growing into a young lady with
relationships of her own.*

Acknowledgments

For Tina Tessina:

Riley K. Smith, for cooperative problem-solving above and beyond the call of duty; and for letting the best book possible be more important than anything else. We've been down a long road together, singing and laughing most of the way.

My husband and support team, Richard Sharrard, for living the attitudes set forth here, and for being my primary support, encouragement, and team member. For the past 20 years, he has been a miracle in my life.

Maggie and Eddie Bialack, Joan and Bill Mueller, Sylvia and Glen McWilliams, Ron Creager, Isadora Alman, Deni Loubert, and David Groves, dear friends who support, encourage, love, and keep me loving life. I am continuously grateful for their love and support.

My secretary, Ruth Campbell, who recently retired after 15 years—patient, painstaking, calm, competent, willing, and reliable. Her work made my work easier.

The tremendous resource of writers that is ASJA: someone there always has the answer.

My recharging places: Beverly's Vintage Tea Leaf and Cindy's The Coffee Cup.

For Riley K. Smith:

I started my adult life believing that, because I alone am responsible for my life, I had to do my life alone.

Developing and working with the material in this book was a part of my learning that, although I'm responsible, I don't have to do it alone.

I want to acknowledge with love and appreciation a few of the key members of the team that created *How to Be a Couple and Still Be Free*:

Tina Tessina, my longtime friend and colleague, who shared in the creation of this material and who patiently taught me a new way to write.

Rhoda Pregerson, who has practiced being Free Partners with me since 1985.

For Riley and Tina:

We want to acknowledge with love and appreciation a few of the key members of the team that created this new edition of *How to Be a Couple and Still Be Free*:

Our students, readers, and clients, who are both the reason and the primary resource for the information and exercises in this book. Thanks for teaching us.

Laurie Harper, our agent, who knows everything we are afraid to ask about contracts, publishing, and royalties. Laurie, you're a pleasure and a treasure to work with.

The Career Press team: Ron Fry, President and Publisher, for wanting to update this book. Stacey A. Farkas, Editorial Director; Kirsten Beucler, Marketing Coordinator; Jackie Michaels, Publicity Director; Kristen Mohn, Editor; and Design Concept for their excellent work and cooperative attitudes.

Those who have supported and believed in this book in the past: the late Al Saunders, Jeremy P. Tarcher, Jean Stine, and Denton Roberts, M. Div, MFCC.

Table of Contents

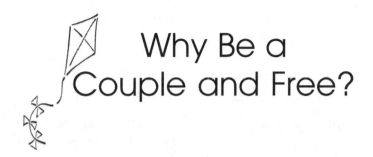

Why Be a Couple and Free?

Why did you pick up this book? Are you intrigued to think it is possible to be a couple and still be free?

How can you be true to yourself and true to your partner at the same time? If you honor yourself, will your partner leave? Can you and your partner have a loving, committed relationship without compromising or without each of you giving up some of who you are and what you need? Is commitment a type of bondage? Isn't it selfish to insist on having what you want? Doesn't true love mean that you joyfully give everything to your beloved? Does having freedom mean having affairs?

You are not alone in your questioning. Most of the people who come to us for help with their intimate relationships are struggling with questions such as these. If you are competing to find satisfaction in your intimate relationships (as so many couples we have worked with do), you may be struggling with your partner while searching for a way to be happy together.

* You may have experienced a sequence of relationships that were destructive and didn't work.
* You may be with someone new and fear you will repeat old, painful patterns.

* You may have a basically good relationship with some specific problems (such as financial struggles, disagreements
  about parenting, sex, intimacy, housework or time schedules) for which you can't find a satisfactory solution.
* You may fight all the time and are unable to resolve even
  minor family problems or conflicts without a painful and
  exasperating struggle, which leaves one or both of you feeling hurt, angry, resentful, deprived, cheated, or frustrated.

These are common couple problems. Sustaining a long-term intimate relationship with a partner is difficult. If you have had experiences
such as these, you may believe that you have to choose between taking a
stand for yourself and having a committed relationship, because you can't
have both at the same time.

We have found that you most certainly can have both. Not only can
you have both, but when you feel free to speak up and say what you
want, confident that you will be heard and confident that your partner
will work with you to find a solution, the love will flow more easily
between you. That is the purpose of this book.

This New Expanded Edition

In 1980, when *How to Be a Couple and Still Be Free* was first published, it introduced a radical concept: cooperation instead of compromise or competition. When one partner compromises needs on behalf of
the other, it invariably leads to a troubled relationship. One partner becomes a resentful caretaker, while the other feels oppressed and belittled.
One partner will be alert to the moods of the other—often walking on
eggshells not to upset the other. One will threaten to leave in order to get
his or her way. One wants more together time and the other wants more
space, and neither is satisfied with the compromise. The compromises
and self-abandonment demonstrated here lead to resentment, hurt, and
power struggles.

When partners struggle, the flow of love between them can be
blocked—even when they truly love one another. On the other hand,
partners who have the tools to negotiate and who are committed to

equality and mutual satisfaction are far more likely to create the love and partnership they deeply treasure.

In the more than 20 years since the book was first published, we have developed many tools and techniques couples can use to create cooperation and freedom. We have expanded this edition to include many step-by-step instructions and guidelines, and we've added the Negotiation Tree, a tool that can help you turn any struggle into a cooperative problem-solving session. Through the addition of these components, we have created a manual you can use to create or restructure your current partnership into a Free Couple Relationship.

Couples and Freedom

Because we aren't talking about having affairs or "playing the field" when we use the word "freedom," and we aren't thinking of any lack of commitment to each other when we say "couple," it is necessary to define both terms. Because these are the terms that attracted you to this book, we invite you to check our definitions against your own. Knowing what they mean to you will better enable you to create the kind of relationship that fits exactly who you are.

What We Mean by "Couple"

As a *Newsweek* special report put it: "The American family does not exist. Rather, we are creating many American families, of diverse styles and shapes. In unprecedented numbers, our families are unalike. We have fathers working while mothers keep house; fathers and mothers both working away from home; single parents; second marriages bringing children together from unrelated backgrounds; childless couples; unmarried couples, with and without children; Gay and Lesbian parents. We are living through a period of historic change in American family life." The trouble is that many relationship books offer patterns and role models based on this nonexistent "American family" and do not adequately consider these other types of relationships, or they do not recognize the changes that have taken place.

How to Be a Couple and Still Be Free is designed to help you create a relationship that is suitable for you, whether your relationship is gay or straight; traditionally monogamous; or nontraditional, such as an open relationship; a group marriage; a bi-coastal, two-career relationship; or a committed, living-separately relationship.

More people are choosing not to marry, or not to stay married, today. Instead, they are redefining couple relationships in many ways. There are many possible variations of satisfying relationships, and this book is about creating the kind of relationship that satisfies you *and* your partner, whether you are married or not. Therefore, we offer a broad definition of "couple" so that you and your partner can use the tools here to develop your own mutually satisfying definition, which is specific to your individual relationship.

We define a couple as two people who are committed to being with each other more intensely and/or more often than with others. This usually implies a degree of love and intimate contact. It could be a dating relationship, living together, married, or not married. It could be a deep, intimate, and sexual commitment, sexually exclusive or not. Our intent is to help you and your partner develop a relationship that is mutually satisfying by your own, unique, and specific definition. With specific, step-by-step techniques and guidelines, this book will teach you the negotiation and communication tools and skills you can use to create a relationship that ensures that both of you get what you want. In short, a relationship that is secure and committed, but within which you both feel free.

What We Mean by "Freedom"

By its very nature, freedom is defined differently by each individual. Each person has individual needs for closeness and personal space, as well as other needs to feel nurtured, understood, and autonomous within a relationship. Individual people define their freedom in very different ways: Some want the freedom to be close and comforted, others want the freedom to be autonomous and unfettered.

Understanding these components of freedom requires self-knowledge. To know what you need, you must focus on your self, see yourself as clearly as possible and accept what you find there. Knowing what you want and what you feel are skills that are essential to creating a mutually satisfying intimate relationship.

In this book, you'll find specific exercises designed to help you clarify what you want and feel, to create a personal definition of freedom, and to communicate that to your partner. By learning and using these techniques, you'll create a mutual understanding and cooperation in helping each other get exactly what you want.

Whether your reasons for wanting to be a couple are romantic or pragmatic, social or cultural, based on passion or a need to create a healthier family than you grew up in, a desire to have children, simple loneliness, or a spiritual or "soul mate" connection, it is important to you, and we want to help you create it as you see it.

The Desire for Intimacy

Most couples are drawn to enter relationships because of the possibility of intimacy. Intimacy, or lack of it, is also what creates most of the struggle in relationships. Creating a satisfying couple relationship requires meeting the individual intimacy needs of each partner.

You need intimacy just as you need food and shelter. Just as with the other basic needs, no one needs intimacy all the time, but some people need more than others. It is possible to be intimate without being a couple; however, the development of emotional closeness over time combined with the easy availability of physical closeness, make couple relationships the ideal opportunity for intimate contact.

Building intimacy is easier in a relationship because it takes less energy and decision-making to get together. Friends, family, and culture support and endorse your togetherness. When things go well, the teamwork of partnership (common goals, successfully solving daily problems, and doing chores together) creates a feeling of mutuality and appreciation that enhances your closeness. As a couple, you are freed from the search for intimacy, so you can focus on other areas of your lives.

In a healthy relationship, intimacy grows with time. Two people who have been together for 20 years can have a deeper connection than they did when they were only dating for three months. Time together doesn't guarantee intimacy, but it does create an opportunity for intimacy to grow. It takes time to know and trust each other. As trust builds, you open yourselves. Over the months (or years), you reveal yourselves.

If you nurture your closeness through the years of each partner's personal growth and changes, you will know more about each other than anyone else, and your contact will grow deep.

Once you learn the communication and problem-solving skills in this book, you'll know how to create the kind of teamwork and mutual benefit that supports the growth of intimacy and satisfaction: a relationship of equal partnership and autonomous cooperation.

Cooperative Problem Solving

Most people don't believe that it is possible for a couple to be so adept at solving problems together that both of them are fully satisfied. The myth is that you must choose between intimacy and freedom—that is, you can have what you want, or you can be close. Couple relationships are seen as an extension of other types of competition. Because this competitive attitude is so ingrained in each of us, it usually takes a shift in belief and a lot of practice to learn how to stop fighting, arguing, and insisting you are right; or to stop being afraid you won't get what you want.

The Free Couple

Free Couples embody five qualities: 1) love easily expressed, 2) mutual respect, 3) a sense of equal power in the relationship, 4) the willingness and ability to express desires, needs, satisfactions, and 5) the willingness and ability to resolve conflicts cooperatively—without power plays, manipulation, and unsatisfying compromises.

How to Be a Couple and Still Be Free will teach you to work together to create whatever kind of relationship you want, free from the restrictive patterns of your parents, your past experience, and social pressures.

When you and your partner know how to cooperate to solve problems and resolve differences, you can freely express your desires, needs, and satisfactions. You can share your worries and your joy without fear of being manipulated by them. You both feel equally empowered. You can say what you want, knowing you will work together to make it happen. When you experience and express mutual respect, love flows more easily between you. You are equal partners. Equal. Partners. You understand how to cooperate to create a truly satisfying life as two free individuals working together. You can be a couple and still be free.

Emphasizing Function Rather Than Dysfunction

Many books have been written about relationship problems. These books place an emphasis on dysfunctional, codependent relationships; compulsive or obsessive love; domestic violence and sexual molestation. They focus on the emotional and psychological (and often physical) damage these relationships cause, how to recognize them, and how to free yourself from them. Simply recognizing, describing, and suggesting ways to end such negative relationship dynamics is an enormous task.

All of these books focus on unsatisfying or unhealthy relationship patterns and how to recognize and overcome them. Little is said about how to create and sustain a healthy, functional, non-codependent relationship. You may be very familiar with the frustration of being told how not to create an unhealthy relationship, but it may never be clear what you should do instead.

So, if you're asking, "What is a healthy, functional relationship and how do we get one?" *How to Be a Couple and Still Be Free* is designed to answer your questions and teach you (either individually or together with your partner) how to create and sustain a fully functioning partnership between equals.

How to Be a Couple and Still Be Free is a manual that provides intimate partners with a proven, step-by-step guide for working together as a team. Together, you can overcome negative relationship patterns and master the positive new skills you'll need to know to create a successful, satisfying, and sustainable relationship that fulfills both your individual needs. The exercises in this book have been used and recommended by many therapists to help couples in therapy.

How to Be a Couple and Still Be Free is a guideline for transforming an unsatisfying relationship into a loving, sustainable, healthy partnership between equals who support each other and work together cooperatively to ensure that each partner gets what he or she wants. We call this equal, mutually supportive partnership a Free Couple Relationship.

The central idea of this book is a method for Cooperative Problem Solving that involves both partners working together as a team. Through this process, any problems, difficulties, obstacles, differences, or struggles that arise can be identified, negotiated, and solved to the mutual satisfaction of you and your partner.

This book will lead you, individually as well as together, through a series of carefully planned exercises designed to help you develop the skills (such as problem-solving, cooperation, clear communication, and teamwork) that will enable you to use the Cooperative Problem Solving process to build and sustain a healthy relationship.

In *How to Be a Couple and Still Be Free* you will learn how to work together smoothly to solve the very problems that created competition, pain, and struggle between you and your partner in the past and to build teamwork and cooperation where you previously had fighting, frustration, and despair. Your problems are probably solvable; relationship problems feel overwhelming and difficult only if the partners involved lack the skills they need to solve them.

The basis of this approach is the Negotiation Tree: A step-by-step guide to working smoothly together to solve all the problems and disputes partners can encounter over the course of a relationship. It will guide you safely through the five steps of solving any problem and help the two of you reach a solution that is wholly and non-competitively satisfying to you both.

This book will introduce you to a relationship of equality:

* Designed to meet your unique needs as individuals and as a couple.
* In which both partners feel equally important, equally powerful, and equally free to express their wants and needs.
* In which both partners work together to find a mutually satisfactory way to get what both of you want every single time.
* In which you support each other in making sure you are both satisfied in the relationship.

* Which contains far less conflict, frustration, anger, and fewer arguments, disputes, and feelings of deprivation than most couples experience.
* Which is easy to sustain because you both learn how to get what you want from it all the time!

How the Book Is Organized

The first chapter, "How to Be a Couple and Still Be Free," explains what an intimate partnership between equals is, why it works so well, and how you can achieve it. Cooperative Problem Solving is also introduced and explained, along with the Negotiation Tree, a step-by-step guide that you can follow through the Cooperative Problem Solving process. The Negotiation Tree will help you much the same way we help our clients, by outlining and guiding you through the five steps of the process, referring you back to the proper information and exercises whenever you have difficulty, and helping you to know when you are ready to go on to the next step.

The next five chapters correspond to the steps of the Negotiation Tree: "Define and Communicate the Problem" (Chapter 2), "Agree to Negotiate" (Chapter 3), "Set the Stage" (Chapter 4), "State and Explore Wants" (Chapter 5), and "Explore Your Options and Decide" (Chapter 6).

These chapters explain each step, why it is important, what happens if you don't cover that step in negotiating, and the problems you may encounter in that step. It provides information, exercises, and guidelines that teach you skills for overcoming each problem as it arises. Each chapter presents examples of couples engaged in negotiating in order to demonstrate how your new skills will work. Each exercise builds on what you learned in previous exercises, so your familiarity with and competence at using the skills of Cooperative Problem Solving will increase as you go along.

The final chapter, "Feeling Free Within Your Partnership," outlines ideas for using Cooperative Problem Solving and the Negotiation Tree to improve various aspects of your relationship, and thus, over a period of time, it will transform the relationship into one that is wholly satisfying to both of you, which will enhance your pleasure in being together and make your relationship easy to sustain.

Using the Exercises

We recommend that you begin by reading this book in its entirety to gain an overview of the stages of the Negotiation Tree and the relationship skills that accompany them. You may be tempted to use the Negotiation Tree right away to solve a problem. If you do, you could find yourself feeling lost and frustrated. Without reading the rest of the book, you might not have enough understanding of what is meant by many of the suggestions and steps of the Negotiation Tree.

The exercises in this book are designed to teach every skill needed for and explore every barrier to achieving a healthy relationship. The exercises build on each other, with the later exercises drawing on skills you learned in prior ones. Each exercise is prefaced with a complete explanation of what it is designed to teach, and when it might be needed in your relationship. Step-by-step instructions help make the exercises easy to follow and easy to put into practice.

Each exercise will supply criteria for determining when you have either mastered each skill, or when you still need more practice. If you find you need help with certain skills, or you need help at a particular point in your negotiation, the Negotiation Tree will refer you to the proper exercises and examples. You can pause in your negotiation at any time to revisit a needed exercise or to help you overcome any difficulty or confusion you're having, and then return to the Negotiation Tree for the next step.

If you have read other self-help books, had couples' therapy, or participated in workshops, some of the skills presented here may already be familiar to you, and you may go on to those that are less familiar or more needed. We have included exercises you can do on your own, as well as exercises you can do with your partner. We recommend you do the exercises in the order they are presented because they build on each other, and they follow the Cooperative Problem Solving process. The exercises themselves will refer you to other related exercises that might be helpful. We have written this in the sequence we feel will meet the needs of the broadest number of readers, but each couple has individual negotiating strengths and weaknesses, and the Negotiation Tree will help you adapt the guidelines and exercises to your own unique situation. Experiment with the Negotiation Tree, and as you use it, you will see which techniques you and your partner most need, and which guidelines are most helpful.

The Negotiation Tree is a "negotiating road map" to the five steps of Cooperative Problem Solving. Once you feel you understand the steps of the Negotiation Tree, the book will guide you to try using it on a simple "practice" problem. Both of you will be astonished to discover how easy it is to use and that the two of you can find a solution where each of you will get what you want!

By the time you have mastered all the skills and exercises taught here, you will have a full set of "tools" that will enable you to fix any problems that may arise in your relationship, before you and your partner are so frustrated and angry that your problem becomes too big to handle.

By reading this book, doing the exercises, and following the Negotiation Tree, you will give yourself the best possible chance of creating a relationship you can both enjoy, feel proud to share, and in which you will feel comforted and supported.

We invite you to open the following pages and begin building your Free Couple Relationship.

Chapter 1

How to Be a Couple and Still Be Free

In 15 years of working with couples in private therapy and workshops, we have found that no matter how unsolvable a problem seems to the couple presenting it, when we help them apply Cooperative Problem Solving, a solution can always be found. Over the years, even when a couple presented the problem that had caused a previous divorce or breakup, we could find at least one solution acceptable to both of them by using the Negotiation Tree. As experts in problem-solving, we know how to help each couple explore all the underlying wants; break free from old, problem-creating behaviors; and eliminate the false limitations they had placed on the problem.

We have found, repeatedly, that most of the trouble that occurs between intimate partners happens because they don't know how to work together to solve problems. The frustration, resentment, anger, disappointment, and despair these couples feel almost always stems from not being able to get what they want from the relationship and from each other. Whether their fights are about money, sex, affection, time, infidelity, in-laws, raising children, housekeeping, or other problems, their inability to reach a mutually agreeable or satisfying solution keeps them repeating the same old arguments without any resolution. It also keeps them locked into habitual ways of reacting with what they think they "should" do. Those actions only create more dissatisfaction and struggle between them.

As therapists, we spend a great deal of time teaching couples the skills they need (communication, cooperation, knowing and saying what they want, overcoming destructive habits, breaking out of rigid patterns that don't work, counteracting "shoulds," and creating new ideas) to solve problems together successfully, and teaching them how to work together as a team rather than struggle against each other. We also spend time guiding people through the process of problem-solving in order to keep them on the track and prevent them from sliding back into their old habits.

If you are like most of these people, you have probably entered relationships madly in love, convinced that your feelings for each other were so strong that they would carry you through into a Free Couple Relationship in which, you would:

* Give and take equally, with each partner feeling equally responsible and equally rewarded by the relationship.
* Be committed to mutual satisfaction. If one of you is not happy, the other really wants to solve the problem.
* Face problems rather than avoiding them, confident that you have a range of proven techniques and skills to resolve any disagreements, struggles, and conflicts that occur.
* Seldom have to compromise, because you work together so that both of you get what you want.
* Feel like a team, working together to maximize your power, instead of competing and undercutting your collective efforts.
* Treat each other's feelings, wants, and needs as important.
* Share thoughts and feelings freely, knowing that positive interaction adds energy to the relationship, and negative thoughts and feelings indicate a problem, which you are confident you can solve together.
* Encourage each other and recognize you need excitement as well as comfort and security.
* Feel comfortable, satisfied and stimulated, so you have little incentive to seek out others or begin again with a new relationship.

* Have confidence that your relationship will last, because problems are solved as they arise, and not allowed to persist and linger until they breed resentment.

Perhaps your past relationships failed to live up to these dreams because, after a short time, your relationship ran into problems, which you did not know how to handle. This is the case with Carol and Joe.

Carol and Joe

Carol and Joe were sweethearts in high school, who married young with the support of both their families. They had a "dream relationship" and high hopes for happiness. Now 35, and a working wife, Carol has spent most of her adult life taking care of others—especially Joe—but feels unworthy of receiving attention, and doesn't realize that it is equally important to take care of herself. Meanwhile Joe, a 38-year-old blue-collar worker, has trouble showing affection, and because he isn't demonstrative and supportive toward Carol, she feels depleted and unresponsive toward him. It doesn't take long for them both to feel deprived and neglected, and their relationship becomes an unsustainable situation. Neither of them can maintain their good feelings toward each other when they feel so deprived, yet both, being insecure, feel that the survival of their relationship depends upon maintaining their roles.

Similar to Carol and Joe, you may have had relationships that frequently felt more like nightmares than dreams. You may have found yourself and your partner struggling with individual wants and needs that differ. Because you didn't know how to work together effectively to solve the conflict, the resulting frustration, anger, and battles made the relationships more and more unpleasant and difficult to sustain.

The fact is that most relationships we observe—those of our parents or our friends, in the movies, and on TV—aren't working very well. They seem to be full of struggle, pain, boredom, and fraught with problems:

* One partner gives and the other takes.
* One is an addict, alcoholic, or a compulsive gambler and the other pays the price.
* One partner overpowers, coerces, defrauds, deceives, or takes advantage of the other.
* They both follow rigid roles that seem to alter or stifle their personalities.
* One gives up a career to support a spouse who succeeds, then leaves.
* Both partners seem consumed with anger, contempt, hostility, or hatred for the other.
* Both compromise their needs for the survival of the marriage.
* They both withhold their true thoughts and feelings because "it would hurt my partner," and feel dissatisfied.
* One or both are numb, depressed, or detached, and they are partners only in that they cohabit, or they stay together "for the children" or because they feel they "have to."
* The romance is gone and there is no vitality.
* Their sexual needs and differences seem to conflict, creating emotional suffering for both.
* One or both have affairs to fill a missing ingredient in their partnership.

Contrary to what you may have seen in your own relationships and others, struggles such as these are not inevitable. There is hope. Cooperative Problem Solving (and the Negotiation Tree) can help you learn to create mutually satisfactory solutions to problems such as these by working together to ensure each other's satisfaction. If the problem is too severe or long-standing to be solved by mutual discussion, the Tree will direct you to seek help, while simultaneously showing you how to make room in the relationship for individual differences, preferences, and tastes.

You can have a successful Free Couple Relationship even when one or the both of you still have some unresolved personal emotional problems. Working together, you can help each other overcome individual problems (whether they are emotional, from past history, work-related, or stem from some other part of your separate lives), and you can make enough room in your relationship that your moods and personalities can coexist without undue struggle. As you develop more mutuality and cooperation, your sense of inner equality will grow and further enhance your relationship in an ever-increasing spiral.

Cooperative Problem Solving offers you an easy-to-follow, effective, noncompetitive method to help you work together to:

* Recognize and solve problems in your relationship, whether you've been together for a long time, or you are a newly committed couple.
* Keep your individual problems from creating partnership problems.
* Solve each other's individual problems to your mutual satisfaction.
* Solve your relationship problems to your mutual satisfaction.
* Review the interaction in your past relationships to learn what went wrong, identify behavior and beliefs that got in your way before, and correct them.
* Identify old relationship patterns that were dysfunctional, addictive, or abusive, and then develop a means for healthy interaction.
* Discuss changing or conflicting individual moods and feelings, or different needs for intimacy, and find ways to accommodate them.
* Identify and examine the "traditional relationship" models to see what aspects of them are relevant to your partnership, and what you need to change.
* Develop a model for partnership, no matter what your style, orientation, or preference, that works for you and your mate.

* Learn the skills you need to be whole, healthy, independent individuals who have satisfying, loving intimacy as equal partners.

Decision-making: It Takes Equals to Solve Problems

There is a pervasive myth that somehow happy couples just agree on everything, automatically, all the time. Because we believe this myth, we enter relationships convinced that whatever problems or differences we have with our partners, they will be easy to solve. But in reality, the individuals who make up a partnership will disagree frequently and often struggle over even minor issues.

In the course of building and sustaining a lifetime relationship, we are bound to encounter many problems. Our different backgrounds and experience; our individual perception of each other and events; our unequal rates of education and growth; our individual needs for self-expression and contact; and our differing values and beliefs about relationships complicate and often block our attempts at Cooperative Problem Solving. Complicating things even further is the fact that models of healthy, effective problem-solving between partners in a relationship have been rare to nonexistent. For centuries, the accepted models for intimate, business, and political relationships were patriarchal and authoritarian with a parental "boss" (usually male) in charge who made all the critical decisions and passed them down to subordinates (often female) who accomplished them without question.

Although competition may work in business, relationship models based on the idea that one person must lead and the other follow, or one person "wins" and the other "loses" become power struggles where the partners fight bitterly when they disagree. They either struggle to be in control, or they avoid disagreements altogether because they feel it isn't worth the struggle, or they wouldn't win anyway. Hence, they spend a lot of their time either fighting for what they want, or feeling deprived. You may have witnessed your parents, friends, or neighbors interacting in this way because in the past, relationships such as these were the norm.

Competition

The belief that someone has to "win" in a relationship encourages us to compete rather than to cooperate. As children, when the teacher favors a brighter student, or a sister who is more aggressive gets to decide the game to play, we learn that if we aren't the best, don't fight hard, or manipulate, we don't get what we want. This leads us to either fight to win, or give up.

Partners try to "win" because they believe in competition, where only one person gets what he or she wants. Most of us are used to competing for jobs, sports, dates, and we even compete with ourselves, to see if we can outdo our previous efforts. When competition is stimulating, motivating, and fun, it is healthy. Between partners in intimate relationships, however, competition becomes stressful, counterproductive, and toxic: poisoning the relationship by turning us into adversaries, and undermining the mutual support and encouragement vital to becoming a Free Couple.

Fear of Difference

There is another reason we often have difficulty resolving problems and conflicts with our intimate partners, where we handle them clumsily, or even poorly. In a relationship intimate enough that we feel a deep bonding or sense of commingled identity, we experience a strong tendency to view disagreements as threatening. Disagreeing seems to indicate that we are separate individuals who perceive everything differently and who have different needs and wants, and we fear that we'll be rejected or disapproved of if we are different.

Problems Outside the Relationship

Sometimes relationship problems are only indirectly connected to your partnership: your car breaks down, your kids need to get to school, or your boss is difficult to get along with. These issues become partnership problems because you bring their effects, big and small, home (into the relationship) with you. Anger at your unreasonable boss can quickly become a difficult evening with your partner if you bring your frustration home, are irritable, and the two of you wind up arguing unnecessarily.

While this feels unfair and inappropriate, it happens frequently in real life. A couple unskilled at working together to solve problems could easily become tangled in a web of blaming, hurt, and anger and, after years of similar unresolved conflicts, can build a backlog of bitterness that can't be healed.

Problems Within the Relationship

Sometimes problems are directly related to your relationship: You fight about housework, money, or you have conflicts over sex. One or both of you becomes hurt or angry. At these times, if you have no method for cooperative negotiation, the conflict and resulting negative feelings can easily escalate into a big problem or accumulate over time. When problems cause friction and never get resolved, they undermine an otherwise loving and viable partnership.

Struggling with your partner and believing that you both can't have what you want prevents you from Cooperative Problem Solving. You may believe that you can't get what you want because you think:

* There isn't enough to go around.
* You don't deserve it as much as your partner.
* It will be taken away from you.
* If you get your way, your partner will go away or be angry.
* It isn't nice to say what you want.

When disagreements or difficulties arise, if you feel hopeless, panicked, angry, or confused, you can't think clearly enough to solve the problem.

Effective Decision-making

Only recently have psychologists and sociologists begun to discuss the elements of effective decision-making. Among other discoveries, they found that decision-making (even in business) is more effective when *everyone* contributes their views of priorities, needs, wants, goals, and their thoughts about possible solutions. This cooperative approach means that both partners contribute their understanding to the problem (which often makes it clearer), both feel involved in the process, and both are committed to the success of the solution they agree upon.

If, up to now, you viewed negotiation in a relationship as a struggle or a hassle, an opportunity to be overpowered or cheated, you are not alone. Because we live in a competitive society where a great deal of emphasis is placed on winning or losing a conflict, it is difficult to realize that, when we are dealing with those we love, problems can be solved through cooperative teamwork and that *solutions can be reached where no one loses, and everyone benefits.*

This book includes an effective and proven model for resolving the difficulties you will inevitably experience as a couple in an intimate relationship. The approach is Cooperative Problem Solving and you may find it revolutionary. The unique aspect of Cooperative Problem Solving is that both parties attempting to resolve a conflict or make a decision can negotiate so *that both get what they want.* The following chapters will help you learn all the highly effective decision-making skills you need to solve each relationship problem as it arises. You will learn how to solve the problems of the past (I'm afraid we'll fight about money like my first wife and I did); the present (I don't think I'm getting a fair share of the housework); and the future (What will we do if I lose my job?). Instead of being a struggle or something to avoid, solving such problems will become an opportunity to reaffirm your mutual love and caring, and to strengthen your partnership and teamwork.

How to Be a Couple and Still Be Free is essentially a step-by-step guide to help you learn how to move easily together through the five steps of Cooperative Problem Solving, using the Negotiation Tree presented later in this chapter.

Cooperative Problem Solving

Cooperation simply means working together as equals, focused on solving the problem in a way that satisfies both partners' needs. Cooperative Problem Solving means you solve problems by working together as equals rather than struggling with each other, so all of your emotional, mental, and creative energy can be focused on creatively exploring the problem, developing alternatives, putting your mutually chosen solutions into action, and solving the problem.

You may think that's a lot to promise because the idea that the two of you can work together to get all that you want *every time* runs counter to conventional wisdom and perhaps to your own personal experience.

Experience and training leads all of us to believe in scarcity and competition. Because our world offers few examples of cooperation, and many examples of competition, winning, and losing, as couples we tend to approach problem-solving in the same competitive way. When we want different things, we argue over which of us gets our way insisting on our being "right" or on making the other person "wrong." Or we just give up convinced it is not worth it or we are convinced that we can never win over our partner and this causes us to feel restricted, deprived, hurt, and angry. This is especially true in relationship problems. When things go wrong, it is easy to believe that there's not enough of what you want to go around.

> Carol and Joe, for example, have a conflict. They both want the car for the evening. Because of their conflicting wants, they get anxious that there might not be enough transportation for the two of them, and begin arguing. Carol (after arguing for about 20 minutes about who needs or deserves the car more) gets angry enough to grab the keys and take the car, leaving Joe to find other transportation. Carol has "won" the car, but created a bigger relationship problem: Joe ends up feeling deprived and angry and Carol feels anxious and guilty. Because they are convinced there is no way both of them can have what they want, they get upset and fight, so neither of them considers an alternate solution, and someone has to do without transportation.
>
> On the other hand, if Carol and Joe learn Cooperative Problem Solving, they will know how to work together as a team to reach a solution that is mutually satisfying. Confident that their goal is that *both* of them be content with the result, Carol and Joe will be much less likely to approach

the transportation problem with a "win or lose" attitude, and both will find it much easier to be flexible, accepting, and understanding of the other's position.

Using their new Cooperative Problem Solving skills, Carol and Joe focus on finding a way for both to get transportation for the evening. They consider other options: Joe can get a ride with a neighbor, relative, or friend; Carol can drop Joe off on her way; either can take a taxi, bus, or a train; someone else may let them borrow a car; they can adjust their schedules so they don't need the car at the same time; or they might even decide to rent or buy another car. They can negotiate until they both are satisfied.

The negotiations you will learn in this book will not prove you're wrong and your partner is right, or vice versa, because the main purpose of cooperation is to avoid the competitive "win or lose" attitude that requires that *someone* has to be wrong. These negotiations are based on the belief that both of you are right and deserve to have what you want.

Cooperative Problem Solving is a new way of looking at decision-making, agreements, communication, power-sharing, and solving problems. It is a new way that can be used to replace the competitive interaction in your intimate relationship with teamwork and cooperation, and the fear that you will "lose" what you want with the confidence that both of you can be satisfied. At first, this cooperative approach may seem radically different and even foreign to you, but you will find it makes sense as it is presented in the Negotiation Tree, and is very effective. As others who have used these ideas and exercises, you can create teamwork and equal partnership in your intimate relationship.

By following the five steps of Cooperative Problem Solving, you will learn a method of resolving conflict based on better understanding each other's wants and needs, communicating clearly, developing new, creative options, making decisions, and reaching solutions that are completely satisfactory to both partners. Cooperative Problem Solving will help you master the basic attitudes and skills of cooperation *at the same time* as it helps you to solve your problems.

Cooperative Problem Solving also motivates you and your partner to participate equally and actively in resolving struggles because the goal of Cooperative Problem Solving is *always* to develop a solution that is *completely satisfying* to *both* of you. Cooperative Problem Solving minimizes confusion by teaching you specific options, such as how to clarify and communicate the problem, how to make sure your partner is equally involved, and what to do when your partner doesn't want to cooperate.

If you cooperate to solve problems when they arise, the experience of working together and caring about each other's wants (Joe and Carol mutually decide that Carol will drop Joe off, so they both have transportation) builds trust and goodwill between you. This feeling of trust (the next negotiation about the car will be easier, and Carol and Joe will be more relaxed because they cooperated this time) and confidence that you can successfully meet challenges together creates a solid bond between you, and is the key to establishing a Free Couple Relationship.

Cooperative Problem Solving will help you solve problems:

*   When you know what you want, but you're not getting it.
*   When you and your partner seriously disagree over what you want or how to handle a problem.
*   Each time you have a partnership decision to make, from buying a new car or house to deciding whose career move is most beneficial.
*   If you know you're unhappy, but aren't sure what you want.
*   If your partner is obviously unhappy and you don't know why.

As you read through the chapters and do the exercises, you and your partner will quickly see which negotiation problems arise most often for you, which skills you need to practice, and which attitudes have kept you stuck in your past relationship problems. As you practice the skills and follow the guidelines in the Negotiation Tree, you will overcome barriers, correct old, competitive attitudes, and develop new skills for communicating. Cooperative Problem Solving techniques will become easier and flow more as you use them.

Barriers and Skills

As you begin to learn and work with the five steps of Cooperative Problem Solving, you will learn many new skills, and probably encounter a number of difficulties that will tempt you to give up and abandon the process. We call the difficulties that arise the "barriers" to Cooperative Problem Solving, and each chapter outlines the typical barriers (such as not knowing what you want, competing, inexperience and mistrust, confusion, lack of communication, not enough information, and unresolved anger) you are likely to encounter at each step of the process. Each chapter teaches you specific skills (such as clarifying your wants, cooperation, reassurance, clear communication, research projects, and discharging old anger) designed to overcome these barriers. For each barrier that arises, the Negotiation Tree will teach you and your partner the skills you need:

a)   To be aware of the possible barriers.
b)   To anticipate them and minimize the problems they cause.
c)   To overcome the barriers you do encounter as you learn Cooperative Problem Solving.

Cooperation and the Free Couple Relationship

A Free Couple Relationship is the long-range benefit of learning to problem-solve in this way. After you and your partner have used Cooperative Problem Solving to work together to resolve several problems in a totally satisfying way, you will begin to feel more secure about your teamwork, and therefore, your partnership. Knowing you can make agreements that both of you will keep, and that when problems arise you can work together to solve them, will build a deeper level of trust between you—trust that you can handle life's difficulties, problems, and disagreements in a spirit of cooperation; trust that you both are willing to work for your mutual satisfaction; and trust that you really care about your mutual happiness.

The communication and negotiation skills that you develop by using the exercises and guidelines of the Negotiation Tree will overlap into the rest of your activities (at work, dealing with children, and relating to other family members and friends). You will discover that the same techniques that make it easier to work together with your partner also ease all other attempts at communication. When you learn how to present a problem clearly in a way that invites your partner to work on it with you, you will be able to use the same method to address a problem with coworkers. Conflicts resulting from misunderstandings will be rare and, when they do arise, far more easily resolved in all areas of your life.

Over time, this new way of relating as equals who work together can transform your relationship, as it did with Joe and Carol.

> They realized through Cooperative Problem Solving that Joe needed to learn to take better care of himself and Carol, who knew how to care for Joe, was learning to be aware of her own needs. As they learned this new mutually caring attitude through solving simple problems such as who got the car, their way of being together changed. At first, Carol asked for more affection and help with the housework. Joe agreed and asked for help learning what she wanted so he could be warm and caring toward her, and to take more responsibility around the house.
>
> As they negotiated successfully through a long series of small adjustments over a period of months, they also modified how they behaved toward each other. Joe learned to share his dissatisfaction with his work, and be more affectionate toward Carol, and Carol felt more responsive and generous to Joe as she learned how to get her own needs met. As a result of working together on these and other related issues, Joe was encouraged to get training for a new, more satisfying and better paying career, and Carol became more independent, and had more time and energy for her career. They learned to cooperate on housekeeping chores, until they became successful enough that they hired a housekeeper.

Their mutual support and lack of struggle at home gave them an extra boost in their careers, both of which thrived as a result.

Couples who know from experience that they can successfully make decisions and feel mutually satisfied and enhanced by being with each other, do not doubt their relationship or their commitment. When a relationship goes well, the reasons for being in it are clear: Why would anyone want to leave a relationship where they get what they want all the time? The Negotiation Tree can help you work together until you develop a habit of seeking mutually satisfying solutions to every problem that arises, so you can build this kind of solid, reliable Free Couple Relationship.

Some people are afraid of commitment and caring deeply, because they're trying to avoid the pain of the loss when it ends. Creating a Free Couple Relationship is reassuring because the ease of negotiation and the openness about wants mean there will not be any surprises. If one of you is unhappy, you will have the tools to talk about the problems, and most likely fix them.

Nothing can protect you from inevitable loss of your relationship someday. No matter how happy you are together, eventually, one of you will probably survive the other. Where there is deep love, deep grief is unavoidable. We believe that being able to experience years of a deep, loving partnership that works is worth the pain of loss at the end.

The Negotiation Tree

STEP I: DEFINE AND COMMUNICATE YOUR PROBLEM.

Is the Problem Clear to You?

If yes,
State your problem to your partner, get confirmation that it is understood, and proceed to Step II.

If yes,
Discuss problem until it is defined, then proceed to Step II.

If no,
Can your partner help you clarify the problem by discussing it?

If no,
Do it yourself by:

1. Doing the Problem Inventory (Chapter 2, page 61).

2. If still unclear, read Chapter 2, Define and Communicate the Problem (page 51).

3. If still unclear, do the Clarifying Your Wants Exercise (Chapter 5, page 181).

4. If still unclear, get help from a friend or therapist.

EXAMPLE OF STATING PROBLEM:

"I'm feeling neglected and needy lately because you're gone so much."

STEP II: AGREE TO NEGOTIATE.

Do You Both Agree to Negotiate?

If yes,

Proceed to Step III.

If no,

1. Reassure your partner or ask for reassurance for yourself, as appropriate. Follow the Guidelines for Reassurance (Chapter 3, page 113).

2. If still no agreement, review Chapter 3, Agree to Negotiate, and do the Trouble Shooting Guide (Chapter 3, page 135).

3. If still no agreement, persist using the Guidelines for Gentle Persistence (Chapter 3, page 132).

EXAMPLE OF ASKING TO NEGOTIATE:

"Will you sit down with me and help me solve this problem?"

The Negotiation Tree (cont'd.)

4. If still no agreement, solve it yourself using the Guidelines for Solving It Yourself (Chapter 3, page 146).

STEP III: SET THE STAGE (THREE PARTS)
   A. Choose a Time and Place

Do You Both Agree on a Time and Place?

If yes,
Proceed to Part B.

> EXAMPLE OF CHOOSING TIME AND PLACE:
> "Is now a good time?" or "How about Saturday afternoon? We can send the kids to the movies."

If no,
1. Use the Establishing Goodwill Guide (Chapter 4, page 156).

2. If still no agreement, reaffirm your agreement to negotiate (see Step II) and try again using the reassurance and communication skills outlined in Chapter 3.

   B. Establish Goodwill.

Have You Both Established Goodwill?

If yes,
State your goodwill and proceed to Part C.

> EXAMPLE OF EXPRESSING GOODWILL:
> "I love you a lot and it's important to me that we enjoy our life together and that's what this negotiation is for."

If no,
1. Use the Establishing Goodwill guide (Chapter 4, page 156).

2. If goodwill is not forthcoming, check for held hurt or anger (Chapter 4, page 161), and, if necessary, follow the Set Aside Held Hurt and Anger Guidelines (Chapter 4, page 165).

3. If goodwill is still not forthcoming, let a day or two pass and start over again.

4. If goodwill is still not forthcomng, see a relationship counselor or therapist.

The Negotiation Tree (cont'd.)

C. Reassure.

Are You Both Confident of the Outcome?

If yes,
Proceed to Step IV.

> EXAMPLE OF EXPRESSING
> REASSURANCE:
> "I want to be sure that both
> of us get exactly what we want
> out of this negotiation."

If no,
1. Reassure each other.

2. If reassurance isn't working, follow the Guidelines for Reassurance (Chapter 4, page 158).

STEP IV: STATE YOUR WANTS
Are You Each Clear About Your Own Wants?

If yes,
Proceed to stating your partner's wants.

> EXAMPLE OF STATING WANTS:
> Partner A: "I want more time for us to be together—at least one more evening a week. I want to know I'm loved no matter what."
>
> Partner B: "I want to work on my projects, be with you and work out at least twice a week. I want to know I'm loved no matter what."

If no,
1. Do the exercise on Clarifying Your Wants (Chapter 5, page 181).

2. If still unclear, let a day or two pass and review the Problem Inventory (Chapter 2, page 61), then with your problem clearly in your mind, redo the exercise on Clarifying Your Wants.

Are Both of You Clear About Your Partner's Wants?

If yes,
Write them out to be certain and proceed to Step V.

If no,
1. Follow the Guidelines for Sharing Wants (Chapter 5, page 191).

The Negotiation Tree (cont'd.)

EXAMPLE OF RESTATING YOUR
PARTNER'S WANTS:

Partner A: "You want to work
on your projects, be with me
and work out at least twice a
week. You want to know you're
loved no matter what."

Partner B: "You want more
time for us to be together—at
least one more evening a week.
You want to know you're loved
and appreciated.

2. If still unclear, use the Abundance
Worksheet (Chapter 6, page 208).

3. If still unclear and you seem to be
stuck, go back to Step III and establish
goodwill and reassure. Then try again.

STEP V: EXPLORE YOUR OPTIONS AND DECIDE (FOUR PARTS)

A. Establish Options

Are You Both Ready to Establish Your Options?

If yes,

Choose the option that you can
agree upon following The Guidelines
for Deciding (Chapter 6, page 218),
and proceed to Part B.

If no,

1. Explore options by expanding
boundaries using The Abundance
Worksheet (Chapter 6, page 208).

2. If no option is suitable, do The
Brainstorming Exercise (Chapter 6,
page 201).

3. If no option is suitable, explore
wants some more using The Abundance Worksheet (Chapter 6, page
208).

4. If no option is suitable, reassure
using The Guidelines for Reassurance if necessary (Chapter 4, page
158). Then start with expanding
boundaries again (A.1 above).

The Negotiation Tree (cont'd.)

5. If you agree on an option and are unsure of its viability, agree to research using The Guidelines for Doing Research (Chapter 6, page 212).

6. If no option is suitable, take a day or two off and come back to it. Review this Negotiation Tree and repeat any parts necessary (for example, *Is this the best time and place to do this? Do we need to reestablish goodwill? Is someone needing reassurance?*).

7. If no option is suitable, it is possible that the issue being negotiated is a symptom of a deeper problem that can only be resolved with the help of a professional counselor. It's okay to get outside help, if necessary.

EXAMPLE OF SELECTING
AN OPTION:
"We'll combine being together with working out. We'll take a racquetball class together on Tuesday nights. We reaffirm our unconditional love."

B. Confirm Your Decision

Each of you state the option(s) selected so that you know you are agreeing to the same option(s).

Are You Both Clear on Your Decisions?

If yes,
Follow the Guidelines for Confirming Your Decision and proceed to Part C.

If no,
Using your communication skills, analyze your concerns and go back to Part A for more exploration.

The Negotiation Tree (cont'd.)

EXAMPLE OF CONFIRMING YOUR DECISION:

Partner A: "We'll take a racquetball class at the health club so we can be together and work out too—and our love isn't conditional. We love each other—together or not."

PartnerB: "We'll combine being together with working out. We'll take a raquetball class together on Tuesday nights. We reaffirm our unconditional love."

C. Writing Your Agreement (optional)

Follow the Guidelines for Confirming the Decision (Chapter 6, page 219) and proceed to Part D.

EXAMPLE OF YOUR WRITTEN AGREEMENT:

1. "We will register for a racquetball class on Tuesday nights at the health club beginning in two weeks."

2. "We will be together Tuesday nights and weekend nights for sure and other times as often as we can."

3. "I love you whether we are together enough or not. I love you and appreciate you no matter what."

signed _____

signed _____

D. Celebrate

Follow the Guidelines for Celebration (Chapter 6, page 225).

Learning to Use the Negotiation Tree

Although the five steps of Cooperative Problem Solving are simple, you will feel awkward when you are beginning to learn to use them. Until you are thoroughly familiar with this new way of negotiating, there will be many occasions when you will not know what to do or will fall back into unhealthy, old patterns such as competing, arguing, not knowing what you want, misunderstanding each other, or feeling discouraged or confused. At such times, you will need help in staying focused on Cooperative Problem Solving, or you may find that your negotiation winds up in argument and frustration rather than solving the problem.

The Negotiation Tree (pages 38-43) is a blueprint for problem-solving that will help ease you through difficulty and speed you back on the right track. Use it is a road map to help guide you through the problem-solving process. You will want to refer to it often, so we suggest you photocopy it for easy reference.

Steps to Cooperative Problem Solving

As you can see on the Negotiation Tree, there are five main steps to Cooperative Problem Solving:

> *Step I: Define and Communicate the Problem.* In this step you'll learn how to clearly define what is bothering you and communicate it to your partner in a way that will make it easy for them to hear, and encourage them to cooperate in solving it.
>
> *Step II: Agree to Negotiate.* In this step you'll obtain your partner's agreement to work together cooperatively to solve the problem to your mutual satisfaction.
>
> *Step III: Set the Stage.* In this step you'll create a relaxed, uninterrupted atmosphere conducive to working together calmly and effectively.
>
> *Step IV: State and Explore Wants.* In this step both of you discover what you want relative to the problem, and work to communicate your wants to each other.

Step V: Explore Your Options and Decide: In this step you'll learn to brainstorm to create new, innovative ideas for solving the problem until you have selected a mutually satisfactory solution. Then you confirm your solution in order to eliminate any possible confusion, and celebrate your success.

For each of the five steps, the Negotiation Tree will ask you to carry out a part of Cooperative Problem Solving such as "define the problem," and then refers you to the section and page in the book that explains that step. So, if you don't remember what that step entails, or you get confused or "stuck" and need help, you can look up the description of that step. The information on page 38 will tell you, in detail, exactly what you must do to "define the problem."

The Tree will ask you a yes or no question; such as: "Is the problem clear to both of you?" and gives you two options (the possible answers to the question. If the answer to the question is yes, you follow the instruction in the yes column: "If yes, state problem, and proceed to Step II." If no, the Tree will tell you what to do: "If no, do The Problem Indicator Inventory (page 61) until the problem is clear, and try again." In this way, the Negotiation Tree will lead you, step by small step, through the negotiation process, and any time a step doesn't work (that is, you get a no answer), it will direct you to the page where you will find the appropriate exercise or guideline that you need *at that moment* to solve the problem cooperatively.

The Negotiation Tree is a set of sequential instructions for Cooperative Problem Solving derived from a time-tested procedure. It points out each step in the procedure in sequence, with instructions and examples of what to do at each step, when to go on to the next step, and when to refer to the exercises and explanations in the book because a step is not complete. The Negotiation Tree is designed as a teacher for beginners and as a troubleshooting aid for more experienced negotiators. In this way, the Negotiation Tree leads you, safely and step by small step, through the entire process.

How to Begin

We strongly recommend reading the book and doing the relevant exercises *before* using the Negotiation Tree, so that you will have a basic understanding of the terms, guidelines, and skills before you use them for the first time. Once you have familiarized yourselves with the tools taught here, whenever you need to solve something, you can begin by following the Negotiation Tree, and allowing it to show you the most appropriate and needed exercises, guidelines, examples, and sections of the book for your situation. It becomes a road map for problem-solving.

When you have read the book, done the exercises, and feel ready to try Cooperative Problem Solving, we recommend that you select a problem that seems simple and straightforward. A small problem that doesn't have an emotional charge and seems easy to resolve will give you a chance to learn the process. Try a problem that you normally just let one person decide without negotiation, such as which movie to see or where to eat, only this time agree not to compromise, and negotiate with the intent of both of you getting exactly what you want through Cooperative Problem Solving. Because the Negotiation Tree helps you focus on creative, new ideas, you may find that you will go out dancing or to a play or concert instead of a movie, or pick up food from two different restaurants and rent a video, so each of you can have different things at the same time!

In the beginning, keeping the problem simple gives you a chance to learn how problem-solving works. Problems such as "What shall we do this weekend?" or "Who does the dishes tomorrow?" are more likely to be successful first-time experiences than emotionally laden problems such as "We're not having enough sex," that have been long-standing and frustrating to either one or both of you.

Run through the process several times over the next few days, practicing with small problems. When you get stuck, use the Negotiation Tree as your guide to the relevant exercises and instructions. When negotiating small problems becomes easy, challenge yourselves by choosing a slightly tougher problem to negotiate. If you've chosen a problem that proves too tough, either break it down into several, simpler problems, or go to a different, easier problem for more practice, (as Suzie and Mike do in the following example) then come back to the tougher problem again.

Suzie and Mike

When Suzie and Mike negotiate about spending money and find that there is not enough money for both to do what they want to do, they could struggle, argue, or fight over who gets what they want. Instead, they realize that they have an opportunity to work together if they break their negotiation down further, from who gets to *spend* the money to negotiating over how to *create* more money.

As they work together to resolve their money problem, they might find hidden resources, alternative and inexpensive ways to have what they want, and that their lack of money is temporary—a minor inconvenience—and begin to plan to create the extra money they need.

Negotiating is not difficult or painful, but in the beginning, learning a new skill can feel awkward and clumsy. Until you get as familiar with the process as Suzie and Mike are, you may occasionally get "stuck" or confused while experimenting. This is to be expected, and the Negotiation Tree will tell you what to do if this happens.

As you begin to experiment, you'll see the steps are simple and easy to understand, and a little experimentation will convince you that the process works. *The only way you can fail at Cooperative Problem Solving is to quit before you learn all the essential skills this book teaches.*

With a little practice, you'll find it soon becomes quite comfortable and easy. The goal of cooperation is to make negotiating a pleasant and successful process. In a relatively short time, it can become second nature to negotiate as a partnership; the success rate you will experience when you try cooperative negotiation will be very rewarding.

It is worth taking the extra time to learn this now, because once you become an expert at Cooperative Problem Solving, it will make problems easy to solve for the rest of your life, and it will give you the confidence to try working together on problems you always thought were impossible to solve. After a few months, you'll be negotiating many aspects of your relationship, until it becomes fully satisfying, easily sustainable, and you both realize you have developed a Free Couple Relationship.

From their experience of cooperative negotiating, Free Couples know the effectiveness of working together to solve problems and the good feeling of teamwork that enhances their goodwill and trust so they face every disagreement, struggle, problem, or question with the belief that it can probably be solved in a mutually satisfactory way. They know that the only solution that will really work is a *cooperative solution*, because a competitive, win/lose solution will undermine their partnership.

This new approach to solving problems works precisely because it is so rewarding. When both of you have enough experience at Cooperative Problem Solving to realize that *you can't lose*, you will approach disagreements, problems, and discussions with a new sense of confidence. You will soon see that each problem-solving session adds new strength and resilience to your relationship because it adds to your conviction that *together you can work anything out successfully*.

Once you learn the process, you will consider no problem solved until *you both get exactly what you want*. You will view each other as helpmates, or team partners, who enhance and add to each other's ideas and options. *The more problems you solve, the stronger your bond becomes.*

If Your Partner Isn't Cooperating

Although ideally you and your partner will use the Negotiation Tree together, unlike most methods of improving your relationship, you can use the Negotiation Tree to learn better relating and communicating skills and solve relationship problems by yourself. There may be times when you understand Cooperative Problem Solving, are clear about the benefits, and your partner is suspicious, uninterested, unavailable, or unwilling to try.

The idea of negotiating may sound intimidating and scary to your partner until you both try it, and he or she may be hesitant to cooperate at first, but we have provided for that contingency. The Negotiation Tree shows you exactly how to take the pressure off your partner and yourself, and make Cooperative Negotiation very inviting to your mate (Guidelines for Solving It Yourself, page 146).

One of the unique features of the Negotiation Tree is that it shows you how to be clear about what your problem is, communicate it more effectively to your partner, and persist in a way that increases the possibility of enlisting your partner in Cooperative Negotiation. By reading the book by yourself, even if your partner is uninterested so far, you can still learn Cooperative Problem Solving and how to make cooperation attractive and inviting to a partner. If your partner resists negotiating, the Negotiation Tree will direct you to the guidelines on Gentle Persistence, which will give you instructions for maximum effectiveness in inviting him or her to cooperate with you.

If you are reading this book on your own, begin with finding a simple problem, defining it so you understand it, and practicing how to state the problem clearly, try Cooperative Problem Solving even though your partner doesn't know about it. Announce to your partner that you need some help with something, and then define the problem. Ask if your partner will help you to solve it and negotiate with you. As the Negotiation Tree says, if you get a yes answer, proceed according to the tree. If you don't, solve the problem for yourself, *but announce to your partner what your solution is, and that you're still open to negotiation if your partner is interested.* This maximizes your partner's incentive to join in and work together with you. This will show your partner the benefit of getting to be part of the solution, even if they know nothing about Cooperative Problem Solving.

> **If Suzie keeps putting Mike off when he wants to talk about budgeting money, Mike can decide he's going to get a separate checking account so he can at least control his share of the money, and invite Suzie to discuss it with him if she has a different idea.**

If You Are Single

If you are single, and preparing for a future relationship, you can use the Negotiation Tree to help solve your problems by learning to use Cooperative Problem Solving with friends and family. Knowing how to clearly communicate what's important to you, to accurately understand what a prospective partner wants and needs, and to be able to work out differences cooperatively, will prepare you for the relationship you want, and help you achieve it smoothly and successfully. When you do find the partner you hope for, having these skills will enable both of you to develop a Free Couple Relationship from the beginning.

After deciding on a simple, beginning problem, copy the Negotiation Tree and begin with the first step, "Define Your Problem," which is fully explained in the next chapter.

## Chapter 2

Define and Communicate the Problem

The Negotiation Tree begins with a simple instruction: Define the Problem. This first step in negotiation may seem very obvious, but its function is to make sure that you understand what the problem is thoroughly enough to clearly communicate that there is a problem in a way your partner can hear and understand. Still, many couples' problems remain unsolved because, while one partner believes the problem is obvious and self-evident, the other partner is confused or unclear about what's wrong, or even unaware that there *is* a problem at all. Even when both agree there is a problem, they often cannot get the problem clearly defined so that both partners understand it or agree on it, they don't communicate well (or at all), or they disagree about what the problem is, as in the example of Rose and John, below. You may have had an experience similar to Rose's:

Rose and John

Rose is a housewife, in her 40s, whose three children are grown (the youngest is in high school), who feels depressed and unhappy. For the last 25 years, Rose's whole life has been focused on making her home pleasant, and caring for her children and husband, which was a full-time job. Now, gradually, her major role has become obsolete. The children are young adults and don't need her very much, and her husband, John, a lawyer, is away much of the time in his high-powered career. Rose is unhappy, but she has trouble understanding why. She tries to talk to John.

Rose: *John, I don't know what's wrong, but I feel bad.*

John: *Gee, I'm sorry to hear that. Why don't you go to the Doctor?*

Rose: *No, it's not that. My health is okay. I just feel listless and tired.*

John: *Are you getting enough rest? Maybe you're just recovering from the flu you had last month.*

Rose: (giving up) *Yes, I guess you're right.*

John: *Get some rest, and you'll feel better.* (ends discussion, goes back to the work he brought home)

Rose indeed has a problem, and one that will profoundly affect John if she becomes severely depressed or despondent, but neither of them can get clear enough about what the problem is. John tries (more than some spouses might) to be supportive and caring, but he hasn't enough to go on, or the skills to find out more (and, subconsciously, he may really be afraid to know). He dismisses the problem, Rose gives up (she feels hopeless about fixing it anyway), and no negotiation takes place. If Rose and John cannot define what the problem is, there is no way they can begin to solve it. The problem is allowed to grow, to become more deep-rooted, and to create all kinds of little secondary problems:

* Because Rose is depressed, she doesn't do housework or cook, and John becomes angry.

* Rose feels so miserable, she is easy prey for an affair with a con artist who uses her and discards her, leaving her with massive guilt and even more depression.

* Rose is so depressed, she doesn't respond sexually, so John is tempted to have an affair.

* Rose uses alcohol, food, or shopping to blunt her pain, and

creates all the havoc associated with addiction: emotional, physical, and/or financial.

In this way, a relatively normal, simple problem, because it was not clearly defined, and therefore could not be solved, can become a major catastrophe and even the cause for divorce.

When you are aware that something is wrong, defining the problem helps pinpoint and clarify exactly what is upsetting or uncomfortable, which makes it possible to communicate. And communicating clearly to a partner makes discussion of the problem possible. Surprisingly, couples often find that defining the problem is all they need to do to solve it, because once both people understand what the trouble is, the solution often becomes obvious.

> For example, if Rose can clarify her problem enough in her own mind so that it is clear when she defines it for John, things go very differently:
>
> Rose: (determined to communicate) *John, I feel bad, I have some ideas about why, and I need your help and understanding.*
>
> John: *Gee, I'm sorry to hear that. I've got a lot of work to do tonight, but I'll help if I can. What's wrong?*
>
> Rose: (she's thought a lot about it) *I've been very listless and tired, and I've thought about it, and I think I'm sad because I don't feel needed enough any more.*
>
> John: (not getting it) *Don't be silly, hon, I need you. I wouldn't know what to do without you.*
>
> Rose: (not deterred) *Yes, I know you do, but that's not enough to use all my time and talent. My life has changed, since the children are grown, and it's changed much more than yours has. I need to discuss with you what I can do about it. If I don't do something soon, the feelings I have now could cause some big problems for both of us.*
>
> John: (hearing, for the first time, that it's important) *Wow, it sounds important, hon, and I do want to talk to you about it, but I have a lot of work tonight. Can we talk about it later?*

Rose: (making a mental note to bring up the subject on the weekend) *Yes. Now that I know you hear me, I can wait until this weekend to talk.* (Rose now knows they can get to the next step, so she ends the discussion, and John goes back to the work he brought home. They'll continue the negotiation process later.)

Because Rose has taken the time to get clear about what her problem is, she is more able to communicate it to John. She also knows, because she's the one who feels that there *is* a problem, that it's *her* responsibility to follow up and make sure she and John work together on it.

She is determined not to allow him to ignore the severity of the problem or to put her off, and she is prepared to help him understand that, unsolved, this will create problems for him, too.

This step, Defining the Problem, consists of both the mental exercise of getting clear about what the problem is for you (usually the most difficult part) and a communication exercise, in showing your partner three things:

1. That there *is* a problem, whether or not your partner is aware of it.
2. What the problem is, in your opinion.
3. The importance of solving the problem (in other words, how your partner will benefit from cooperatively solving this problem, even though he or she has been unaware of it until now).

Learning to clearly define the source of dissatisfaction or discomfort that first makes you aware of a problem, to communicate it effectively, to invite cooperation, and to recognize when you are being heard are the skills you will learn in this step of the Negotiation Tree.

Barriers to Defining the Problem

Although some problems may be easily defined and communicated (you're angry because your partner isn't doing chores, you don't like the way the two of you interact at parties, you have an investment problem to discuss), you may encounter more difficulty when you attempt to define problems that are more complex or confusing (you have a vague, pervasive unhappiness; you feel neglected or unappreciated; you're not sure how much responsibility each of you should have). This chapter will help you with those times when you have trouble defining exactly what you need to discuss with your partner. For most people, four common barriers arise when they attempt to Define the Problemc: *confusion, rebellion and compliance, "Shoulds," and secret expectations.*

Confusion

Most of us first become aware of a problem because of a vague sense of uneasiness, discomfort, frustration, or malaise. Few of us know, instantly and certainly, exactly what is bothering us, or what to do about it. You may find yourself thinking: "If it weren't for (your partner, your job, the weather, etc.) I'd feel better," or even wondering if you're slightly ill (Maybe I'm coming down with something. I've been working too hard. It must be that time of the month. Perhaps I'm tired).

Sorting through this confusion, learning to be responsive to the inner prompting that says a problem exists rather than ignoring it, and taking enough time to achieve clarity about what's bothering you will make a tremendous difference in your problem-solving abilities. Too often, couples create problems on top of problems by being unclear about what the original difficulty is, or by ignoring discomfort or dissatisfaction until the problem has intensified and grown into overwhelming proportions. The Problem Inventory Exercise presented later in this chapter will teach you how to identify, define, and be appropriately aware of potential problems *before* lack of clarity turns your molehill-sized, everyday problems into mountains.

"Shoulds"

All of us have rules that define who we are, and how we live: things we feel we "should" or "should not" do, such as the 10 Commandments, rules of etiquette, and standards that define behavior as "generous" or "selfish." Some of these rules are well thought-out ideas we have developed from our life experience, and they work well for us. Others are unconscious prejudices and mistaken beliefs we acquired by early training and observation of flawed role models that we have never had cause to examine or change.

We all grow up with ideas of how we "should" be in relationships, what the proper roles for persons of our gender are, and how husbands, wives, and single people must act. No matter why we have these internal "Shoulds," if they are too rigid, they can become limiting, stressful, stultifying, awkward, or problematic; interfering with our happiness and success in life and in our relationships. Believing you "should" do something "just so" or behave a certain way can be a barrier to Defining and Communicating Your Problem, because when your needs, desires, or the reality of your situation challenges or contradicts a "should,"you will feel confusion and guilt as a result. To avoid this discomfort you will suppress or ignore what you really want, and without that knowledge you cannot create a truly satisfying life for yourself.

In the section about "Shoulds," you will learn about *cultural rules* and *family rules* for being who you are, and find exercises to make these rules more adaptable to your life circumstances by turning your "Shoulds" into permissions. These exercises will help you explore the unconscious rules that may be running your relationship, and help you to achieve the freedom of choice you need to create a cooperative and mutually satisfying partnership.

Competition, Rebellion, and Compliance

Because the society we live in values competition, and we've learned to be afraid of losing, being disappointed, or deprived, and because many of us have been taught to believe that it is self-centered, greedy, or impolite to say what we want, it can be difficult to tell your partner that there is a problem, or that you're unhappy. On the other hand, if you are successful in business and used to controlling negotiations, it may be difficult for you to listen and accept while your partner defines a problem. You may automatically jump to the defense, which is a way to win in competition. Approaching problems with a belief that someone wins and someone loses, or that one person is more deserving or powerful than the other, means if you "lose," you don't get what you want unless you rebel by breaking the agreement, procrastinating, or sabotaging. If you choose to rebel, you will feel disruptive, uncooperative, and angry; the relationship will be in turmoil, with fighting and arguing. Your other option is to comply (give up, martyr, be disappointed). If you comply, you will feel powerless, depressed, and eventually enraged. It will feel as if you "lost." Your relationship may seem smooth for a while, but after giving in for a while, your anger can creep out in subtle, passive-aggressive ways (losing sexual desire, being depressed and miserable, getting sick) or in periodic explosions over insignificant issues.

> **If Rose accepted that all problems result in someone winning and the other person losing, she might have assumed that John would "win," and everything would have to stay as it was. Then she might never have brought the problem up until she was so upset, depressed, or desperate that she had to. Or she might have decided that in order to "win," she would have to rebel: get angry and make demands of John, who would then probably react to her attitude and struggle against her. In the first example, Rose did bring the problem up, but gave up easily and complied with what she thought he wanted, feeling she had "lost."**

Neither compliance nor rebellion leads to mutually satisfactory solutions, because one partner always gets less while the other gets more, which leads to guilt, disappointment, frustration, and anger. The exercises in the compliance and rebellion section (page 66) will teach you how to avoid either extreme and instead negotiate as equals, with equal votes and "veto" power, so neither of you feels you have to give up what you want (comply), or declare domestic war (rebel).

Secret Expectations

It is often considerate, gracious, or polite to try and guess what the people around you want and need from you. So, you may have developed that ability well enough that you are often accurate. However, in an intimate relationship, when you make guesses about what your partner wants and needs, and your partner, in return, makes guesses about you, it is very easy to interpret each other's signals differently.

As a result, you and your partner can believe that you have a clear understanding without realizing that your interpretation of the agreement is different.

Sooner or later, someone's expectations will not be fulfilled, because your partner guessed wrong about what those expectations are. Hurt feelings, upsets, and even rage can result. When you feel very confused or more upset than the problem warrants, you and your partner have probably developed a secret expectation, or unconscious set of "shoulds," that can be one of the major reasons problems between couples do not get solved.

The exercises that accompany the Negotiation Tree will help you understand what secret expectations are, how they develop, and what to do about them. When your secret expectations are no longer secret, the source of many mysterious and confusing upsets in your relationship will be astoundingly clear. Once a secret expectation is exposed and understood, it will no longer trouble you.

Don and Dale

Don and Dale, a committed gay couple in their 30s, may think they have a clear agreement about housework. Don thinks his job is taking out the trash, and Dale washes the dishes. Dale may think he is supposed to wash the dishes, while Don waters the plants. Although most of the time everything gets done, for a couple of busy weeks Don doesn't water the plants, assuming Dale will do it. When the plants begin to drop their leaves, Dale accuses Don of "not doing his share around the house." Don, whose been faithfully taking out the trash, even though he was busy, is highly insulted and feels unjustly accused.

They have just experienced the result of an unclear, covert, assumed understanding—a secret expectation. Such expectations can obviously create difficulty and interfere with Defining the Problem because they create confusion, which makes communication difficult.

A secret expectation exists when you make guesses about what your partner wants, and force your partner to guess, by not being open about what you want. Secret expectations are "secret" because no one ever states out loud "I want you to...." or asks, "What do you want?" or "would you like me to...?" In short, no one clearly Defines the Problem. Secret or covert expectations are common in codependent relationships, because the partners try to "read each other's mind," and please their partner by anticipating what he or she wants.

The exercises in the Secret Expectations section (page 79) of this chapter will teach you how to tell when secret expectations are operating and how to bring them into the open so you can clearly Define the Problem, or communicate effectively with your partner. You will learn how to renegotiate them into clear, effective, open agreements.

Exercises for Defining the Problem

The exercises in the Defining the Problem section (listed below) will teach you skills to overcome all four of these barriers, including: *confusion, rebellion and compliance, "shoulds," and secret expectations.*

* *A Problem Inventory:* Will help you define and communicate your needs and wants clearly, so both you and your partner can understand the problem and learn to translate your negative statements (what you don't want) to positive statements (what you want). This overcomes the barrier of confusion.
* *A Compliance and Rebellion Inventory:* Will help you recognize and disarm competition, or compliance and rebellion when it arises.
* *Guidelines for Creating Permission:* Will teach you how to disarm "shoulds."
* *A Rights and Responsibilities Analysis:* Will help you change your secret expectations into open agreements.

With these skills, you will be able to successfully Define and Communicate Your Problem and move on to the next step, the Agreement to Negotiate.

Confusion

Sometimes you know you're unhappy, or that something is wrong, but it is difficult to get a clear enough idea of exactly what the problem is so you can convey it to someone else. In our experience, many people who come for counseling know they're unhappy and that their relationship doesn't seem to be working, but are confused because they do not understand why. So, the first step toward helping to find a solution becomes helping them sort through confusion in order to Define the Problem.

It is quite easy to see that Rose is confused when she first tries to Define her Problem to John. Because she isn't clear about exactly what the problem is, she can't explain it effectively to John, and he, not knowing how important it is, quite nonchalantly brushes the problem (and, incidentally, Rose) off.

Similar to John, most of us are not eager to have a new problem brought to our awareness in the middle of everything else we have to do. Most of us do not go looking for more problems to solve. So, if the problem is unclear, and doesn't sound important, we are quite relieved to ignore it, and the problem doesn't get solved until it grows into a big, unpleasant issue.

To be effective, you need to learn about *how* to communicate problems to your partner in such a way that he or she can hear and understand, yet not feel defensive, overwhelmed, or hopeless about solving them. Good communication will make it more likely that you will have your partner's help in solving the problem, and therefore, the difficulty will get satisfactorily solved.

Defining the Problem includes explaining to your partner why solving the problem is beneficial to both of you, because, until your partner understands the gains to be derived from solving it, it won't seem worth the effort and the problem will seem to be only yours. The better you are at defining it, and making it clear why and how "your problem" will impact on your partner, the more motivated your partner will be to help you solve it.

When you recognize that a problem exists because you are uncomfortable, unhappy, or dissatisfied in some way, but you feel vague or confused about exactly what it is, the following problem inventory will help you define and understand the problem clearly. You can greatly enhance the effectiveness of your communication with your partner if you take the time to list and evaluate the problem indicators and create a clear statement of the problem, because you'll understand what's wrong enough to explain it. A clear explanation will motivate your partner to want to solve the problem because the benefit will be understood, and you'll be able to work together cooperatively to solve problems faster and easier, before they become a source of trouble.

Exercise: The Problem Inventory

To do this exercise, you'll need a pencil or pen and paper, some quiet, undisturbed time, and a comfortable place to be alone, to think, and to write.

Choosing a simple problem to solve will make this Problem Inventory (and also Defining the Problem) easier. But even if your problem is difficult or long-standing, the Problem Inventory will show you how to analyze the indicators that a problem exists, and help you understand why it is a problem for you, so you can communicate it more clearly to your partner.

1. List the problem indicators. *No matter how confused or uncertain you may be over what your problem is, you are aware of it. That means there is some feeling (sadness, anger, confusion), physical sensation (tightness in the chest, a tension headache), circumstance (one of you is procrastinating at doing chores or paying the bills), or interaction with your partner (one of you was critical or angry for no apparent reason) that has made you aware that there is a problem. These symptoms are problem indicators. Confusion is usually caused by a number of conflicting or competing ideas and feelings that are all trying to get your attention at once. By listing the problem indicators, you can see each one individually, and your confusion will lessen. On your paper, make a heading called "Problem Indicators," and write down whatever experience or feeling that first indicated to you that there might be a problem. For example, Rose's list might read:*

Problem Indicators

* *I'm crying a lot.*
* *I feel frustrated.*
* *I feel useless.*
* *There's not enough to do.*
* *I'm eating too much.*
* *Unrealistic fantasy about having another baby.*
* *John seems to be pushing me away.*

List everything that seems to indicate you have a problem, even if they seem too obvious to mention, such as a fight between you and your partner, or too silly, such as a dream or a passing thought that seems connected.

The more complex or long-standing your problem is, the more time you will have had to develop and observe indicators, so the longer your list will be. Taking the time to think about why *and* how *you know there's a problem will also help you to become aware of the less obvious indicators because you'll stop ignoring or glossing over them when you give them some thought. Don't rush this step: Take enough time, at least 10 to 15 minutes.*

If you feel very confused about a particular problem, you may need to take longer on this step, putting your list down for a few minutes, an hour, or even a day or two, and adding to it as new insights occur to you. When you finally think your list includes all the important indicators, go to Step 2.

2. Evaluate your indicators. *Review each Indicator on your list. Look for central themes of emotion, things, or situations: Are your indicators about time, money, power or control, freedom, loss, comfort, sadness, anger, fear, self-criticism, or frustration?*

If there are several items about crying, depression, or loss, the theme would be sadness. If several items are about being rushed, no time to play, or wasting time, that's a "time" theme. Identifying a theme of emotion, things, or situations gives you a way to evaluate and understand the hidden meaning of your indicators _and organize them into categories, which will make the more subtle dynamics of the problem clearer._

Next to each Indicator on your list, write the appropriate theme. If you're not sure what the theme for one Indicator is, put a question mark (?) next to it, and go on to the others. After you get through the rest of the items, that one may be clearer, and you can write the theme next to the question mark. If not, go back to Step 1, and think about it a little more, and see if you can find more indicators that will make the theme come clear. If it's still not clear, put it aside until after you've done Step 3, and concentrate on the items you feel more clear about.

Here's what Rose's list looked like after this step:

* I'm crying a lot (loss).

* I feel frustrated (?) [on second pass] (time, loss, self-criticism).

* I feel useless (self-criticism).

* There's not enough to do (time).

* I'm eating too much (self-criticism, comfort).

* Unrealistic fantasy about having another baby (loss).

* John seems to be pushing me away (loss).

Rose's list is about time (too much on her hands), loss (children grown up, John ignoring her, she cries), and self-criticism (she feels useless, eats too much) from which she needs to comfort herself (eating).

3. Put the themes into a sentence. _Now, below your Indicator List, write the themes you found. Rose's list would be "time, loss, self-criticism." Using these themes, compose a sentence or two that describes the problem. Rose wrote: "I'm experiencing loss because my children are gone and I have time on my hands. Now that I'm not taking care of them and John anymore, I criticize myself a lot, and I feel worthless."_

Rose's problem was important and complex, so she didn't come up with that sentence immediately. She had to think about her themes for a while first, and she also wrote several descriptions before she found the one that fit.

If your problem is simple, and your confusion is mild, (you're annoyed about feeding the dog, and a little confused about whose job it "should" be), listing the indicators and themes may make the problem clear to you very easily. If the problem is more deeply rooted or long-standing, and you have a lot of confusion, like Rose, you will have to think about the themes for a while before you can relate them to each other and express your problem in sentence form. When you have completed your sentence, go on to the next step.

If you have a lot of trouble identifying themes and creating a sentence, put this exercise aside, and do the exercises that follow in this chapter. As you explore your own relationship to rebellion and compliance, "shoulds," and secret expectations, you'll discover what blocks prevent you from clarifying the problem. Then return to finish this exercise.

Note: Once in a while, during this exercise, someone will realize that the confusion is a result of some deep inner problem such as early childhood trauma, an addiction, a deeply entrenched behavior, or severe emotional upset, that is too complex to be solved without help. In that case, take your Problem Indicator list with the themes to a therapist or counselor for guidance.

4. Review for clarity. *Once you have clarified your confusion, and have a description of the problem that you understand, the next step is to make sure it will be clear and not confusing to your partner. Review your descriptive sentence from Step 3 as though you were reading it for the first time, to see whether it's clear enough to be understandable to your partner.*

You may want to say it out loud, or tape-record it, to get the full impact of how it sounds. If you like, you can pretend your partner is sitting opposite you and practice explaining the problem to him or her. Your purpose is simply to Define the Problem, and not to express your feelings. If you let frustration or resentment creep in, and phrase the problem in terms of blaming someone (even yourself), your partner will probably react with defensiveness and confusion, and you won't be able to move ahead in your negotiation.

Keep in mind that you're describing the problem as you experience it. *State it in terms of yourself.*

For example, Rose will be more likely to be heard if she says, "I feel useless and not very important now that the children are grown," than if she says, "The children never call, and you're neglecting me." John can be more sympathetic and less defensive if he doesn't feel criticized or attacked. (If you now clearly understand what your problem is, but you cannot express it without resentment or fear, read the next section, compliance and rebellion.)

Review and refine your statement of the problem until you are ready to communicate it positively to your partner and you feel quite sure your partner will be able to understand it.

5. Learn from your experience. *The final step of this exercise will help you become more sensitive to the signals that tell you a problem exists, which will make recognizing and Defining the Problem easier as time goes on. Review what you've learned about your confusion while you were doing the previous steps of this exercise in order to analyze what your indicators are. For example, a tense feeling in the pit of your stomach, a headache, exhaustion, or depression might be an Indicator that shows up whenever you have a problem, and by becoming sensitive to these recurring signs, you can become aware of unsolved problems much sooner.*

As you do this exercise several times for different problems, you will begin to see a pattern to the problem indicators. For example, Rose often eats too much when she is unhappy, but has not yet defined the problem. By becoming aware of this Indicator, whenever she notices she's overeating, she can immediately take the time to Define her Problem, stop the overeating, and handle the problem while it's still small and manageable.

Your recurring indicators may include butterflies in your stomach, sleep disturbances or dreams, or irritability. Once you know these are just problem indicators they will not be as upsetting, and as you work on Defining the Problem, those indicators will subside. When you've done this exercise many times, it will become quite easy to analyze your problem indicators and Define the Problem quickly, without formally writing them down.

Compliance and Rebellion

Even after you have done the Problem Inventory, and you feel clear about what your problem is, you may find you are still reluctant to approach your partner with the problem, or some difficulty articulating it calmly. If you feel like attacking or blaming your partner or fighting about the issue, or you're reluctant or afraid to bring the problem to your partner, you are probably experiencing either rebellion or compliance. It is another aspect of the win/lose competitive attitude we have talked about before. In this case, the struggle is about who has the power (or is "in charge") in the relationship.

Rebellion is defying someone because you feel he or she is trying to manipulate or control you. Compliance is giving in or trying to placate and please someone whom you feel *has the right or power* to control you.

Both rebellion and compliance are based on the belief that the power between you is unequal, because one person has, or seems to have, more power than the other. Cooperative negotiation cannot take place between unequal partners, because if you are the partner who feels powerless, you will either comply, and not say clearly what is wrong (Define and Communicate Your Problem), or rebel by blaming and accusing your partner instead of communicating your problem.

Traditional relationship styles have often promoted unequal power, leading people to believe that one partner should be "in charge," while the other complies. This power imbalance is implied in such cultural expressions as the title of the old TV series *Father Knows Best*. Because of this traditional model, many couples assume their relationship has room for only one person in charge. But operating this way leaves one partner feeling like a "parent" (responsible, in charge, powerful, needed, generous, abusive, used, overwhelmed, or critical) and the other feeling like a "child" (minding or misbehaving, irresponsible, restricted, pampered, spoiled, hopeless, helpless, or abused). As a result, neither partner feels satisfied, respected, loved as a unique individual, or equal.

Every adult in a healthy relationship occasionally does parental or childlike things. For example, you can comfort each other, either of you may take the most responsibility for a particular chore or situation, or you can both be playful and silly when you're having fun. However, if you feel "stuck" with too much responsibility or not enough power in the relationship, you will respond with rebellion or compliance, which produces friction, tension, and confusion. Consequently, both you and your partner will feel dissatisfied, frustrated, unequal, resentful, and unhappy.

Even when one partner does not intend to be controlling, it is possible to interpret his or her behavior in that way. On the other hand, many people have been known to rebel against or comply with restrictions that are self-imposed and only *projected* onto the partner as an attempt at control or coercion. For example, if your partner says, "I'd like to get up early," you can interpret that to mean, "We have to get up early or I'll be angry," without ever questioning your assumptions.

You may feel that you "should" do certain things in certain ways, because "it's the right thing to do," or "everybody does it this way," or "I'd be embarrassed if we did it that way." If you were raised strictly as a child, now you may be controlling yourself as rigidly as your family once did, and believing the control comes from your partner.

Your partner may not be trying to control you, but by giving in without objecting, *you* make it seem that way. Even if he or she does tend to tell you what to do, it may or may not be intentional, just a habit carried over from the workplace or from past experience. (That is, if your wife supervises a number of people at work, she may continue behaving at home as she does all day toward her employees, giving orders and organizing them. If your husband has had a previous relationship with a passive woman, he may be used to deciding everything, and forget you're more independent.)

Compliance and rebellion often exist, not because your partner is trying to control you, but because *you are expecting yourself* to do things in certain, rigid ways (or not allowing yourself to relax until stringent—perhaps impossible—requirements are met).

In most cases, the unequal interaction that prompts rebellion or compliance is merely based on confusion and old habit patterns, and is quite easily solved by learning cooperative negotiation, which teaches you to solve problems like the equal, competent adult that you are. But if you have a history of being in dysfunctional, codependent, or abusive relationships, or are a survivor of childhood abuse, this issue of compliance or rebellion will be a very big one for you, and you might want to seek counseling to help you learn to protect yourself and maintain your equality.

As a normal, intelligent adult, you have the *capacity to be equal*. If you have not been equal in your relationship, it is because your *inner inequality* has created the outer inequality. Learning to interact as a Free Couple means you will begin by *acting as if* you are equal, and in the process, actually *become* equal partners, carrying your share of the relationship responsibilities, and no more. *Acting as if* begins with learning to Define and Communicate Your Problem.

Exercise: Compliance and Rebellion Inventory

In the following exercise you will learn to recognize when you are acting out of rebellion or compliance, how to discuss your interaction with your partner, and consider and decide what changes you wish to make in your interaction to make it more equal.

If you and your partner are using this book together, each of you can do this exercise separately. To avoid being confused, or having your answers influenced or distorted by each other, do not share or discuss your answers until you are instructed to do so.

The Quiz: *Answer the following questions by filling in the blanks with "always," "usually," "sometimes," "seldom," or "never."*

1. When something needs to be done around the house, I _____ initiate the necessary action.

2. I am_____in charge of how we spend money.

3. I_____feel angry when I am left out of decisions.

4. I_____ find it harder to do something if my partner wants me to.

5. I will_____fight to win an argument even if I know I'm wrong.

6. I_____ feel like a parent, the boss, or otherwise in charge.

7. My partner_____feels like an extra burden or responsibility for me.

8. I_____resist asking for help, or being taken care of.

9. I am_____sure that my partner can't manage things as well as I can.

10. When household chores need doing, I_____double-check to see if my partner is doing what he or she is supposed to.

Rate your answers as follows: 1 point for each "always" or "usually," 2 for each "sometimes," and 3 for each "seldom" or "never." Now add up your score and compare it to the following analysis:

10-15 points: *You won't have a difficult time Defining the Problem or understanding what it is, because you are used to being "in charge," knowing what's wrong, and what to do about it. The problem may be that you will also try to define everyone else's problems for them. You may also have trouble communicating a problem to your partner, or getting his or her cooperation, because you have a tendency to* tell *your partner what the solution should be (which causes your partner to rebel and argue, comply and insincerely agree, or "clam up" and not participate), rather than negotiating and creating the solution with your partner as a teammate. In the following discussion, make an extra effort to listen to your partner's feelings, ideas, and opinions, rather than be so focused on your own ideas and solutions.*

16-25 points: *You feel quite equal to your partner, are more willing to negotiate, and probably pretty evenly balanced between being compliant and rebellious. You value teamwork and mutual agreement. Defining the Problem is fairly easy for you, because you are used to thinking for yourself, and you will probably be able to communicate it well enough for your partner to understand. You will probably enjoy the following discussion, and it will help you build even more teamwork because you will keep an even balance between listening to your partner, and sharing your own thoughts.*

26-30 points: *Even when you have used the Problem Inventory to help you, you will probably have some trouble Defining the Problem because you will have trouble feeling your needs are important enough to bring the problem up to your partner. But, if you allow the problem to go un-negotiated, you will eventually resent the situation and feel unsatisfied and trapped. In the discussion section, concentrate on speaking up for yourself and invite your partner to help you be more assertive about what you want. If you are afraid your partner will mistreat you if you speak up, get some professional help by calling a local domestic violence hotline.*

The Discussion: *With your partner or a good friend, discuss the above quiz as follows:*

1. Compare Answers: *Reread each of the 10 questions in the quiz, compare your answers, and take two minutes each to explain why you answered "always," "usually," "sometimes," "seldom," or, "never" to that particular question. This will help you better understand the ways you rebel or comply, and your reasons for it, which will help you be aware of and correct the behavior as you learn to problem-solve as equals.*

2. Compare Scores: *Compare your total scores, read the appropriate score interpretation paragraphs, and discuss whether you think the evaluation is appropriate for yourself and your partner. If your opinion of your own attitudes of compliance and rebellion differ from what the interpretation says, tell why you think it's different. If your opinion is that the evaluation is accurate, tell why. Now do the same for each other's evaluation. This will also help you understand and be more aware of rebelling and complying. Then you can begin to interact more as an equal with your partner, to improve your communication and problem-solving.*

3. Consider Changes: *Discuss how your power roles (feeling like "parent" or "child"), patterns of compliance (giving in to or placating your partner), and rebellion (blaming, arguing, or fighting back) hinder your problem-solving and communication, and how it prevents you from clearly Defining the Problem and communicating it to your partner. Talk about how you have fought back, complied, or given up in other situations and previous relationships, including your childhood.*

Also discuss situations in which you have discussed a problem as an equally powerful person, and how that helped you work together. Finish the discussion by recapping how your compliant or rebellious attitudes have created problems in the past, and how you can change your behavior (by saying what you want, not agreeing when you don't want to, calmly giving your different opinion instead of blaming or fighting) so you can solve problems more as equals in the future.

Now that you have tallied your scores, and reviewed or discussed your answers, you have a clearer idea of how much you comply or rebel in your relationship. You may be quite surprised to find out how restricted you feel, and that both you and your partner feel restricted in similar or different ways. Knowing how these restrictions have hindered your problem-solving in the past will motivate you to change your old habits of rebellion or compliance and strive to become more equal partners, by learning cooperative negotiation.

"Shoulds": Rules, Customs, and Traditions

Rules for relating that are arbitrary and do not consider your individual needs are called "shoulds," and they can be a major barrier to clearly understanding and Defining the Problem. If you are feeling unhappy, uncomfortable, or frustrated in some aspect of your relationship, and you are having trouble Defining the Problem, you may be in conflict with, or unaware of, your own internal rules for relationships, and how relationship rules work. For example, if Rose believes she "should" be happy and fulfilled as a housewife, she'll have trouble admitting or understanding that she is unhappy because her life lacks meaning.

Children learn how relationships work before they are old enough to be able to judge or evaluate what they are taught. Observations of society, the patterns and traditions in your family when you were growing up, and what you were told as a child combine to form a largely unconscious list of "rules" for being in relationships. Because the rules are learned so early, we are never able to examine them for effectiveness, functionality, and health: we simply accept them as right.

These rules are seldom learned directly; no one explains how you must be in your relationship. Rather, children learn by inference, example, and (often painful) experience. Through approval, disapproval, and example, your family, friends, and partners teach you what is "expected" of you. As a naïve child who believed what you were told, you accepted these rules as facts, engraved in stone: "it's what everybody thinks," or "it's the right thing to do." In fact, these family patterns are often mistaken, outdated, or even destructive and dysfunctional.

Kinds of "Shoulds"

Several types of "shoulds" can be operating in your life and your relationship: *traditional rules* are the social customs that "everyone knows," that you acquired by observing others, and through childhood experience. Though they seem like facts, you'll find that when you look at them closely, many of them seem less logical. Though traditional rules are changing today, most of us are old enough to have learned them as "proper" attitudes and behavior, even if we don't agree with them. You can tell when these "shoulds" are operating because you will use words such as "acceptable," "right," "proper," and "normal" when you think about them. You see society's rules out on the street, on TV and in movies, and when you're at gatherings of people—at a party, at a bar, at work.

They are the "unspoken rules" most people seem to follow and that people are laughed at or looked down upon for not following. Examples of traditional rules are:

* Men open doors for women and allow them to go first.
* Women wait to be asked.
* Don't talk openly and honestly about emotions, sex, or money.
* Lying or denying is better than upsetting people.

Gender stereotypes are a form of "shoulds" that define our roles as men and women in our culture (often according to our ethnic heritage). Even though these roles are changing today, old habits die hard, and many of us were brought up to believe that men "should" behave in one way and women in another, and those ways may not be compatible with who the individual men and women are. The "rules" for your own gender affect your behavior, and those for the other gender affect your choice of a partner, or, if you are in a same-sex relationship, they may affect the roles you take. Some examples of gender stereotypes are:

* Men shouldn't be too emotional.
* Women don't handle money well.
* A single man avoids commitment, a single woman wants marriage.
* A man is responsible in the world, a woman is responsible in the home.

In addition to all these unwritten "shoulds" or rules for behavior within the society, your family had its own expectations. These are messages you received in childhood about how men and women "should" behave: "a lady doesn't sit that way," "big boys don't cry," "the man controls the money in the relationship," "the father supports the family," or "a wife has to make her husband happy." Also, there are family rules you learned from watching what adults did:

* Daddy (therefore all men) yells when there's a problem.
* Mommy (therefore all women) suffers silently.
* It's grown-up and sexy to smoke (drink, drive fast).
* Problems are never talked about, there's just a lot of tension in the air.
* The family is more important than the individual in it.

Rose, who was brought up to believe that women are not supposed to make waves, and are supposed to be fully satisfied within the home, could have a lot of trouble even realizing why she was unhappy, and even more difficulty Defining the Problem clearly enough for John to understand. As long as Rose was content at home, the rule was no problem, but, when circumstances changed, Rose was trapped by her compliance with a rule that no longer fit.

You and your partner grew up in different families, which had their own ways of doing things, and you had different experiences in life, so each of you will have beliefs about how you "should" be in relationships. Whenever your different rules collide, conflict is almost guaranteed. Each of you will feel very strongly that the other is not doing what "should" be done.

> **If Joe's mother was home with him all the time when he was a child, and Carol's mother worked, Joe and Carol will most likely have conflicting ideas (built on their different childhood experiences) about the woman's role in the relationship. Joe and Carol both enjoy (or need) the money Carol's career generates, but when she can't meet Joe's expectations and get home from work before he does, she may be shocked and confused by how resentful or unreasonably angry he is.**

Similar to Carol and Joe, most people are unaware of the "shoulds" that describe how we are supposed to be in a relationship. Social rules can be useful and without some mutually understood guidelines for proper behavior, we would not be able to create an orderly society. But they often cause problems in intimate relationships. Expectations about social interaction and business behavior (such as proper ways to meet new people, good manners, and business decorum) help bring order to our lives and guide us in dealing comfortably with strangers, business associates, and social contacts.

But in intimate relationships, we go far beyond the kinds of interactions (how to address strangers, how to behave at a party, how to conduct a meeting) these social rules address: We become *intimate*, which means we get to know each other's more private selves, and we interact on an *emotional* level, not a social one. To make intimacy work, we must deal with each other as caring individuals. If attempting to guide intimate partnerships with "shoulds" worked well, relationships wouldn't be so difficult and fail so often, and spousal and child abuse would have been eliminated generations ago.

Becoming aware of your traditional, social, and family rules makes it possible for you to clearly understand the difference between what you "should" do, and what will be effective and satisfying. Understanding that "shoulds" are not necessarily functional, and may be in conflict with what you actually need to be happy and fulfilled, can help you whenever you feel locked in a struggle, confused, or unable to solve a problem.

> **Carol believes that, as a woman, she must take care of Joe and his needs before she takes care of herself, so she has trouble realizing when she is overburdened and her depression and anxiety are a result of her stress. Joe has a similar belief that as a man, he shouldn't be concerned about his emotional needs or his own comfort and care. As long as Carol and Joe do not examine these beliefs, they will feel frustrated, unhappy, and "stuck" in roles that aren't working, and that keep their relationship from being satisfying.**

The danger of having unconscious rules is that you will either comply with or rebel against these "shoulds," and never really get to know how *you* want to do it.

"Shoulds" can prevent you from Defining the Problem by:

* Making you believe you shouldn't have the problem.
   Rose may be intelligent and motivated to go to school, but her "shoulds" say she should be a housewife, so she can't have a problem related to wanting more.

* Being inappropriate to our lives as adults.
   As a child, Joe learned not to complain or speak up when he was unhappy, but now it prevents him from letting Carol know what problems they could solve in the relationship.

* Causing you to believe you can't take what is obviously a good solution.
   Carol and Joe could use the extra money, but Joe's belief that women stay home makes him resist Carol's working, even though she wants to.

* Requiring you to deny some of your natural abilities and aspirations.

   John would like to take guitar lessons, but his "shoulds" say that's too frivolous, so he says he's too busy with work.

* Making it impossible for you to communicate, because you have different "shoulds" about how to do it.

   Dale learned that whoever yells loudest wins the argument, Don learned not to talk about it at all, so Dale yells, Don "clams up," and they never Define the Problem.

Understanding that these subconscious rules exist will make it much easier for you to understand why you feel confused, unable, or reluctant to Define the Problem. Whenever you feel stuck, you can search for the "should," or the rule that is restricting you, and in its place Create Permission. This will make it easier to Define the Problem by giving you the freedom to act according to what is actually needed, rather than be limited by rules that may not apply.

Even when both partners agree on some "shoulds," rigid adherence to specific rules doesn't work in the long run, because it is boring and tiring. Circumstances (such as illness, change of job, or business travel) may make it necessary to change behavior from time to time. Having permission to customize your relationship in whatever way works is much more realistic and is the key to having freedom within your couple relationship. Creating Permission gives you the flexibility to be able to adapt your rules when they conflict, communicate more openly and honestly about what's wrong, and therefore, to Define the Problem readily.

Creating Permission

Once you realize how traditional, gender, and family rules for behavior have been preventing you from Defining the Problem, and you know what some of these rules are, the next step is to give yourself permission to change "shoulds" into "coulds."

The easiest way past the barrier of "shoulds" (traditional, family, and gender rules) is to think "I could," instead. That is, you can create permission to either follow, alter, or ignore the "rule." In this way, you can take each "rule" that causes problems in your relationship and change it into a permission, or a choice.

Exercise: Problem Inventory Part 2

Go back to the Problem Inventory *on page 61 , and reread your Indicator list. You may discover that many cultural, family, traditional, and personal rules have added to your confusion and prevented you from seeing the problem clearly before.* One of Rose's rules was: "Women are supposed to be fully satisfied within the home." She rewrote that rule as follows: "As a woman, I could choose to work, go to school, or be a housewife, depending on what I want, and what my needs are."

Following Rose's example, rewrite each of the traditional rules, gender stereotypes, and family rules listed as permissions.

When "shoulds" are combined with communicated expectations, they create confusion and chaos, which makes it very difficult to think clearly enough to define, understand, and communicate the problem: We call the resulting dynamic *secret expectations.*

Secret Expectations

Secret expectations are expectations or assumptions that one person makes and believes the other person "understands" or "knows" without ever confirming them verbally. The one who has the secret expectation may not even realize how important or significant it is because it is often so automatic it's never been examined or thought about. These expectations get in the way of Defining the Problem because they keep the problems hidden.

Secret expectations form quite easily, because most of us make assumptions about the future from what has happened before.

Iris and Jan

If Iris and Jan meet on a Wednesday, and then the next week Jan calls and asks Iris out for Wednesday night, and the following week it happens again, when the fourth week arrives, and Jan doesn't call, what will Iris think? She'll most likely be upset, because she thought they were going out every Wednesday.

What Iris doesn't know, because it wasn't mentioned, is that Jan has a late business meeting every fourth Wednesday night; and Jan doesn't realize that Iris has a secret expectation that Wednesday is their night out. Iris's expectation that Jan would call has led to her believe that something is wrong, that Jan may have stopped wanting to see her, because she doesn't know the facts. Iris will be hurt, disappointed, and possibly upset, and she and Jan may even have an argument over it.

Secret expectations can get even more emotionally loaded when they are connected to "shoulds" left over from childhood.

If Joe expects Carol to make dinner at 6 p.m. every night because that's what his mother always did, that's a "should." If, in addition, he (probably without being aware of it) believes Carol's making dinner on time means she loves him (and conversely, if dinner isn't ready, she doesn't care about him), then Joe has a secret expectation. If Carol doesn't know about Joe's expectation, and he doesn't realize that Carol doesn't think dinner on time is very important, a relationship problem is brewing and will catch them by surprise. Things can get even more complicated if Joe thinks Carol's supposed to put dinner on at 6 p.m. to show she loves him, and she thinks she's supposed to iron his shirts to show love. Carol could be working very hard at ironing shirts to let Joe know he's loved, while he is getting angrier and angrier because dinner is late.

Secret expectations can usually be spotted when you or your partner overreacts to an event.

If Carol doesn't have dinner ready at 6 p.m. when Joe gets home, but leaves a note (on his freshly ironed shirts!) that she went to her mother's for dinner, and there's a frozen dinner in the freezer, he may be very upset. Instead of asking what happened, Joe overreacts to the surprise, throws a fit, and threatens to divorce her. Carol is completely mystified, confused, and feels unjustly accused of not loving him, because all she can see is that he's overreacting to a change in his dinner.

Long-standing resentment is another telltale sign of hidden expectations. If you have hidden expectations of how your partner "should" behave, and he or she doesn't comply (because you haven't let your wishes be known), resentment will slowly build up, sometimes until it is released in a rage.

In our earlier example, Dale might not say anything when the plants are not watered (partner Don doesn't realize it's "his job" in Dale's eyes), and go ahead and water them, but if it happens a few times, Dale will get angrier and angrier, until one day he explodes.

This sort of confusion and the repeated arguments and explosive interaction caused by secret expectations can be a block to Defining the Problem, and detrimental to a sustainable, satisfying relationship.

Changing your secret expectations into open agreements disarms them and eliminates the resentment and arguments they cause, while making it much easier to clearly define problems when they come up. Once the secret is out, and you realize expectations exist, it can be quite simple to make an open agreement. The following exercise will help you become aware of your secret expectations, so you can turn them into permission, and proceed to negotiate wherever you disagree about your expectations.

Exercise: Discovering Secret Expectations

Because the indicators for secret expectations are irritation, frustration, resentment, or any reaction that is out of proportion to what really happened (as when Joe blows up because Carol isn't home to fix dinner), *by reviewing your relationships for these overreactions, you can backtrack to discover what secret expectations are at work.* Carol might look into her past relationships for some clues about why her secret expectation is that she should be ironing shirts.

1. Mentally review your past relationships for "trouble spots." Were there times when your partner got extremely angry, hurt, afraid, or upset about something you did or didn't do? Write a brief (one or two sentence) description of what happened. For example, Carol may write: "Joe got unreasonably angry when I wasn't home to make dinner, even though I ironed his shirts, and told him where I was."

2. Now review your own behavior in those relationships. Were there times when you got upset, angry, frustrated, or disappointed out of proportion to what your partner did or didn't do? Write a brief description. For example, Carol may write: "I got very angry when Joe didn't appreciate my ironing enough. I steamed about it for days."

3. Look at these two lists, and try to imagine what the "should" or expectations were when the overreactions happened. For example, Carol may write: "Joe must have expected that I would always be home to make dinner, and I must have expected that he would appreciate my ironing his shirts enough to not mind getting his own dinner."

4. Turn your expectations into permissions by putting "could" or "can" in place of "should." Carol may write: "I can let Joe know I love him in other ways than by making dinner and ironing shirts. We can talk about what our responsibilities are in the relationship."

If possible, use the above information to discuss your secret expectations with your partner. Seek to discover secret expectations when they exist by becoming aware of resentment and overreactions as they happen. Talk about the "warning signs" you see in yourself and in your partner, the kinds of secret expectations you have had in the past, and what you can do to correct them. When you detect a secret expectation, turn the expectations into permissions, and work out a solution together, using problem-solving if necessary. Discuss how to bring up the subject in a way that can be heard when either of you believes that your partner is harboring a secret expectation.

Secret expectations often arise when partners don't openly discuss the rights and responsibilities each one has in the relationship. Acknowledging these rights and responsibilities, and agreeing on them makes Defining the Problem easier because it helps eliminate secret expectations and the resulting confusion.

Rights and Responsibilities

As partners, you have rights in your relationship (just a you do in our society) and along with these rights come certain responsibilities. For example, partners have a right to have reasonable sexual needs met, and a responsibility to keep a positive emotional atmosphere that's conducive to lovemaking. You also have a right to be clearly communicated with (and listened to) and a responsibility to do your share of the communicating (and listening). But when partners have different "shoulds" about each partner's rights and responsibilities, it can be a barrier to Defining the Problem. If you do not believe you have the right to ask for what you want, or the right to be satisfied, you will not be able to communicate your dissatisfaction to your partner. Couples often make the mistake of *assuming* they know (without stating aloud) what their individual rights and responsibilities are, which leads to having secret, rather than open, agreements. Learning to be aware of, and communicate, your mutual rights and responsibilities helps you create open agreements, and clearly define any problems that arise.

As a Free Partner, you have a responsibility to assume an equal share of the normal financial, maintenance, and social obligations of life, because Free Partners (as we discussed in Chapter 1) are equal partners. That doesn't mean you have to "keep score" and always contribute equally, but that your agreement must feel *mutual*. In addition, you have a responsibility to keep your relationship sustainable: that is, to take care of yourself, to ask for help when you need it (but have other options in case the answer is no), and to cooperate with your partner *as much as you can without resenting, being deprived, or feeling damaged* by what's requested of you.

In a Free Couple, partners' rights include:

* Being able to ask for what you want (and find another solution if the answer is no).

* Saying no to your partner, in order to take care of yourself.
* Doing what you need to do to be happy, healthy, and satisfied.
* Cooperating with your partner in order to create a relationship that you enjoy.

The following exercise will help you analyze the responsibilities in your relationship, and discover your own and your partner's rights. Clarifying your rights and responsibilities helps you evaluate whether you're exercising your rights and meeting your responsibilities effectively. Knowing your mutual responsibilities and rights, and keeping them in balance, will help you define and express problems more clearly, recognize your right to be satisfied in each situation, and also help you understand your partner's point of view.

Exercise: Rights and Responsibilities Analysis

You can do this exercise whether or not you are currently in a relationship, if you do not have a current partner, or your partner is not participating. Fill out the "partner" columns as you think your ideal (or current) partner would fill them out. If you and your partner are doing the exercise together, do the columns alone first in order to give your discussion maximum effectiveness, and do not share your answers until instructed to do so in the discussion section, so that you won't influence each other's answers. You'll need paper and a pencil.

1. Divide a piece of paper in half, lengthwise, by either folding it or drawing a vertical line down the middle. *Head one side of the paper "Me" and the other "My Partner." Under each name, put two column headings: "Rights" and "Responsibilities."*

Your paper should look like this:

Me		My Partner	
Rights	*Responsibilities*	*Rights*	*Responsibilities*

2. Fill in the column headed "Me." *Under "Rights," list all the things you see as your rights as a human being, and your rights in the relationship. For example, your rights might include: "the right to privacy," "the right to feel what I feel," "the right to work when and where I want to," "to decide how the money I earn is spent," "to go out alone with my friends," "the right to ask for what I want," and "the right to be heard by my partner." Take your time and get at least 10 rights listed.*

3. List what you see as your responsibilities in the "Me" column. *Include chores and work responsibilities as well as emotional responsibilities. For example, you might list: "the responsibility to do the laundry," "responsibility to be a responsive sexual partner," "responsibility to earn enough money," "responsibility to keep peace," "responsibility to keep myself healthy," "responsibility to earn the family's living," or "responsibility to say what I want." It's helpful to put related things in both columns, such as "the right to be listened to," and "the responsibility to be a good listener."*

4. In the columns marked "My Partner," repeat Steps 2 and 3. *Do this for your partner's rights and responsibilities,* as you understand them. *For example, your partner may want the right to have separate friends and the responsibility to keep you informed about activities and keep commitments made with you.*

5. Evaluate your own list. *Compare your columns. Does it look balanced and fair to you? For example, do your rights outweigh your responsibilities or vice versa? If not, go back and add rights to balance each responsibility, or vice versa. Do your partner's rights and responsibilities seem about equal to yours? If not, go back and add rights to balance each responsibility, or vice versa.*

Keep adding to your lists, making adjustments until you feel your rights and responsibilities and your partners are approximately equal. Ideally, your rights and responsibilities and your partner's will feel mutually satisfying and reasonable to both of you.

6. Discussion. *With your partner, (or having a friend play the role of partner), compare the lists of rights and responsibilities. Make this an opportunity to increase your understanding of each other and your beliefs about the rights and responsibilities in your relationship. Ask questions about differences you have come up with, acknowledging each other's good ideas, and compare these lists to the actual rights and responsibilities you have in your current relationship. If you find that some of the things on your list are not present in your current relationship, discuss how adopting those rights and responsibilities would change things between you.*

7. Create a mutual list. *After your discussion, create a new list, with the rights and responsibilities of each partner, that you can both agree on. If you find yourselves struggling about a specific right or responsibility, use that as an opportunity to practice cooperative negotiation.*

Taking the time to become clear about your rights and responsibilities in the relationship can give you the confidence to see that you do have rights, including the right to define and speak up about problems. You will also have a clearer agreement about your mutual rights, and the reassurance that each of you recognizes your responsibilities.

3 Elements for Defining the Problem

Now that you've learned how to overcome the barriers of *confusion, "shoulds," rebellion and compliance,* and *secret expectations* that may arise when you attempt to define and communicate a problem to your partner, Defining the Problem will be quite easy for you to do.

As stated in the beginning of this chapter, there are three things to communicate in Defining the Problem:

1. *A problem exists:* The *Problem Inventory* will help you resolve any confusion you have and make you clearly aware that there really is a problem to be solved. The *Compliance and Rebellion Inventory* and the *Rights and Responsibilities Analysis* can also be useful in reassuring you that you have a right to ask for help with your problem, and to strengthen

your resolve to ask for the cooperation you want. By doing these exercises whenever you feel confused, you can learn to be more confident in your knowledge that a problem exists, just as Rose learned to in the example at the beginning of this chapter.

2. *What the problem is:* The final steps of the Problem Inventory are designed to help you become clear about what the problem is. If you still have some doubts or confusion about whether you "should" feel the way you feel about the issue, reread the section on "shoulds" and Creating Permission, and use the Discovering Secret Expectations Exercise to break free from old stereotypes and assumptions that prevent you from seeing it clearly.

3. *Why your partner should cooperate:* In order to make your problem clear to your partner, you may need to explain (as Rose did), that if the problem goes unsolved, it will soon be a problem for your mate, too. The Rights and Responsibilities Inventory, Compliance and Rebellion Inventory, Creating Permission, Discovering Secret Expectations, and Problem Inventory, added to the information you already have about why equal partners have more satisfying relationships, will help both you and your partner understand how both of you will benefit from cooperatively solving a problem, even though one or both of you have been unaware that the problem existed until now.

Once you have Defined the Problem and Communicated it clearly to your partner, you are ready to move on to the next step in the Negotiation Tree: Agree to Negotiate.

Chapter 3

Agree to Negotiate

Once you are clear that there is a problem and you have clarified what the problem is, it is time to engage your partner to work with you to find a cooperative solution for it, to Agree to Negotiate.

Attempting to solve a problem without an Agreement to Negotiate means your intention will be unclear to your partner. If, when you brought up problems in the past, you have found yourself competing, fighting, arguing, doing without, being a martyr, feeling manipulated or exploited, giving in to "keep the peace," or otherwise getting nowhere, it is probably because you began trying to work on the problem without a clear, mutually understood agreement that you'd work together to find the solution. Your partner may think you are complaining, criticizing, or just ventilating.

You can avoid struggling and fighting if you make certain your partner is prepared to work cooperatively with you. Getting an Agreement to Negotiate with your partner means you have a spoken contract that each of you will give your best effort and attention to working cooperatively to resolve the problem you've defined to your mutual satisfaction.

Getting an Agreement to Negotiate minimizes competition and struggling and encourages cooperation between you because it establishes the following important criteria for problem-solving:

1. It establishes that you *are problem-solving* and not discussing, arguing, commiserating or anything else.
2. It makes clear your mutual commitment to work *together* to solve the problem.
3. It is a way of communicating to each other that you are *both participating* in the process of negotiating.
4. It helps you *focus your attention* on the task of solving the problem.

You've probably had the experience of bringing up a problem only to have your partner assume that your intention is to fix blame, decide who is right and who is wrong, get your way at his or her expense, or just generally complain. Without overtly agreeing to negotiate beforehand, you are more likely to argue because your intention to problem-solve is unclear. For example, Michelle, 24, and Lou, 35, struggle over who has the power in their relationship:

Michelle and Lou

Michelle: *Lou, you treat me like I'm a little girl all the time and that's getting to be a serious problem for me.*

Lou: *Well, you act like a little girl. You act so helpless about doing things around the house and about money. What do you expect me to do?*

Michelle: *There are some things you do more easily than I, but that doesn't make me your little girl! There are also some things I'm really good at and you still treat me as if I'm incompetent and unworthy of respect.*

Lou: *What are you complaining about? I pay the rent and I pay for everything when we go out! You want to start paying half of everything?*

Michelle: (defiant) *Maybe I do.*

Lou: *Hah! That'll be the day.*

Michelle never mentioned that she would like to solve a problem, so Lou interpreted her complaint as an attack, responded defensively, and they never got beyond arguing. Michelle's problem of feeling patronized and demeaned is still unsolved (and effectively not communicated to Lou), and although Lou may feel that he "won," Michelle's frustration and anger from the argument will make it difficult for him to get the intimacy he wants.

If Michelle had Defined the Problem and asked for an Agreement to Negotiate, Lou might have felt consulted instead of attacked and therefore, would have been less likely to get defensive, and more able to hear what she was saying.

But arguments can also happen even when one partner clearly offers to negotiate, but the other partner has not clearly *agreed* to join in negotiating. Here Michelle clearly wants to negotiate, and so does Lou, but he is still defensive:

Michelle: (stating problem, taking responsibility for her part, but vague) *Lou, I'm getting more and more uncomfortable about the way you treat me. My behavior and attitude probably has something to do with it, but I don't know what. Can we talk about this and see if we can solve it?*

Lou: *I don't like it either.* (not a clear agreement)

Michelle: (begins restating problem without a clear agreement) *When you tell people that I don't know something or I can't do something, I feel incompetent and uncomfortable. If you would give me credit for knowing what I know and doing what I'm good at, I would feel a lot better.*

Lou: (defensive, not trying to cooperate) *Well, why don't you talk back? Why don't you stand up for yourself?*

Michelle: (beginning to argue) *I don't know. It just seems futile, I guess.*

Lou: *Well, there you are! You just give up! I wish you'd grow up!*

Michelle stated her problem and asked to negotiate. Then she proceeded to discuss the problem as if she had gotten an agreement when, in fact, Lou had not agreed to negotiate. That left Lou free to avoid negotiation by criticizing her.

In order to have an effective, successful negotiation, both of you must be committed to the problem-solving effort. Without a *mutual* agreement, you will probably wind up struggling instead of working together to find a solution.

This chapter will show you how to get an Agreement to Negotiate with your partner, how to be sure both of you are equally committed to solving the problem together, and what to do if your partner won't agree. Because this agreement is the first step toward making a *mutual* commitment to Cooperative Problem Solving, there are more possible barriers to the Agreement to Negotiate than any other step in the process. In learning to overcome these barriers you will learn most of the skills that end competitive struggles and make cooperation possible. This will make using the remaining steps of the Negotiation Tree much easier and speed you on your way toward a truly cooperative partnership. You can see the change in Lou's response when Michelle uses what she learned about Defining the Problem, and gets Lou's agreement before negotiating.

> **Michelle:** (clearly defining problem and taking responsibility for her part) *Lou, I have a problem I'd like your help with. I often feel like you're the one in charge and I'm your little girl. I know both of us contribute to that interaction, and I'd like your help in solving that problem. We're both missing out if we can't be our full selves with each other and act as partners. I think you'd get a lot more of what you want if we worked together as equal adults, and I'd like to see the playful little boy side of you once in a while.*
>
> **Lou:** *And I'm tired of being grown-up all the time. Let's see if we can negotiate this.*
>
> **Michelle:** *Okay.*
>
> Now that Lou and Michelle both understand the problem and have clearly agreed to negotiate it, the chance that they will be equally committed to solving the problem are much greater, as is the likelihood that they will successfully reach a mutually satisfactory agreement.

You don't need to ask for an agreement as formally as Michelle did, but it needs to be clearly communicated and clearly agreed to as in this examples:

> **Fred:** *Naomi, I'm really unhappy about our sex life and you seem to be unhappy lately, too. Let's sit down and see if we can sort this out together.*
>
> **Naomi:** *Yeah, I'd like to do that.*
>
> **Don:** *I'm going to start riding my bike to work on Thursdays so I can save time getting to night class.*
>
> **Dale:** *Don, I think that's dangerous and I'd worry about you. Can we talk it over and see if there's a better solution?*
>
> **Don:** *Okay, I don't want you to worry.*

When you and your partner have a history of success in Cooperative Problem Solving, Agreeing to Negotiate is quick, simple, and usually easy. But, if you are new to the process, or you and your partner have a history of struggling, you come from a family where there was more fighting, rebellion, or compliance than negotiating, it is not unusual for one partner to resist negotiating. You may have trouble getting agreement in the beginning, because your (or your partner's) old, competitive habits will have a tendency to take over. Cooperating to solve problems is a new concept, and because you are new at it, you may feel discouraged, awkward, or worried that you won't do it right.

When partners are hesitant or feel hopeless about solving the conflict, they will not be as motivated to negotiate. Or you may agree, and then not follow through. All of these problems are solvable, and this chapter is designed to show you how to overcome these barriers to making an Agreement to Negotiate with your partner.

Skills for Cooperation

For most people, working *together* to solve conflicts is a totally new concept. Not only does it require a new way of thinking about problem-solving, but it also requires a set of skills that may be new to you.

These basic skills are:

1. Trusting the process of Cooperative Problem Solving and getting past your unfamiliarity with it, instead of letting your old habits take over.
2. Communicating clearly, with *agreement creating* "I" messages, "active listening," and "attentive speaking" instead of *conflict creating* criticism and defensiveness.
3. Reassuring each other, instead of struggling.
4. Persisting gently instead of giving up or getting angry.
5. In the event your partner cannot or will not work with you: Finding your own solution without your partner's help, instead of feeling helpless, dissatisfied, and angry.

Getting an Agreement to Negotiate is the most critical step in Cooperative Problem Solving, because no mutually satisfactory solution can be found if both people are not equally involved. Sometimes, agreeing to negotiate can be the most difficult step to achieve because it is the point at which cooperation begins, and most couples are not familiar with solving problems cooperatively rather than competitively. Because of these difficulties, and in addition to exercises that help you learn the above skills and guidelines that you can use as you work together, we have created the Troubleshooting Guide at the end of this chapter. If you can't agree to negotiate, the guide will help you determine what your difficulty is and how to solve it. Related exercises and guidelines will teach you the skills you need to communicate clearly, understand your partner better, persist gently, and overcome competing and struggling.

Effective Communication

One of the main keys to getting an Agreement to Negotiate is knowing how to communicate effectively. We have placed it first because it is so important, and you will use it in every exercise in this chapter. Effective Communication can help you overcome inexperience and mistrust because you will be able to get across to your partner why Cooperative Problem Solving will be beneficial to you both without causing him or her to feel coerced or overwhelmed. It will also help you become more

Conflict Creating	Agreement Creating
Michelle: *You're condescending to me and I don't like it.*	M: *When you make a joke about something I do, I feel bad.*
Lou: *I'm just joking. Can't you take it?*	L: *Do you feel put down when I joke about you?*
Michelle: *Why are you such a bully? You put me down and when I complain, you put me down again.*	M: *Yes, I do feel bad if you joke about me.*
Lou: *Look, when I joke around, I don't really mean it. You should know that by now.*	L: *I don't mean to make you feel bad, it's just that when you do something absent-minded, I feel like teasing you.*
Michelle: *I think you do mean it. I think you want to punish me for screwing up.*	M: *You feel like teasing me, but to me it feels like criticism. Maybe I already feel bad, so your joke really hurts.*
Lou: *What a bunch of bull!*	L: *Wow, I had no idea it hurt you so much. I'll be more careful about joking. Now, do you want to get back to talking about the problem?*
Michelle: *Forget it. I'm not going to talk to you.*	M: *Thank you. I'll try not to be so sensitive. And yes, let's get back to the housekeeping issue.*

effective at *reassuring, overcoming rescues,* and *persisting,* because all of those skills require communication. In fact, throughout the rest of the Negotiation Tree, because many steps of Cooperative Problem Solving involve talking and sharing, the information and communication skills you will learn in this section can be used to fix many of the problems often encountered in problem-solving. In this chapter you have already seen that *how* you communicate your problem is crucial to being heard.

Here, you will learn communication techniques that will help you:

* Keep your communication cooperative, rather than competitive.
* Reassure your partner when fear blocks your problem-solving.

* Keep your conversation focused on getting information and solving the problem rather than defending yourselves.

The Basics of Communication

Expressing your thoughts and feelings as facts about yourself ("I feel scared" rather than "you scared me") leads to agreement because your partner will be more able to empathize and care about what you feel. Expressing criticism of your partner ("you don't love me") leads to conflict because your partner will feel attacked and defensive. Here are some examples of statements or questions that Michelle and Lou could use in their effort to negotiate about housework. Read the following parallel conversations and feel your reaction to the statements on each side. See if you can understand why we've categorized them under "Conflict Creating" or "Agreement Creating."

While it may seem difficult to make such rational agreement creating statements in the midst of a conflict, you'll see it is not as hard as it looks, and certainly not as damaging to your relationship or difficult as dealing with constant conflict. If you review the conflict creating statements, you will find they exhibit several attitudes:

* *Defensive:* When you or your partner feel attacked, you'll be busy denying that you're to blame, and not listening to each other.
* *Argumentative:* When you focus more on who's right or wrong or denying the problem is real instead of focusing on how to work together to solve the problem.
* *Objecting:* When you counter each of your partner's statements with a counterargument instead of listening and trying to understand, or criticize your partner's opinion instead of listening.
* *Critical Judgements:* When your responses are about what's wrong with your partner instead of what your partner is saying.

All the above attitudes will be more likely to get a hostile, resistant response because they are negative and attacking, which prompts the listener to counterattack. Therefore, the longer this conversation goes on, the more argumentative, negative, and uncooperative it gets.

Both Michelle and Lou have a better chance of reaching an agreement to negotiate with the agreement creating statements in the right-hand column, which have four elements in common:

* They demonstrate that you're listening because they reflect back what the other person said, which is reassuring to your partner, diffuses defensiveness, and invites a similar, thoughtful response.
* They give or request nonjudgmental, factual "I" message information.
* They are short and simple, so they can be easily understood.
* They are calm and thoughtful, rather than dramatic, emotional or reactive.

Because agreement creating statements are calming, reassuring, and informative, knowing how to use them in your negotiation can help you reduce the length and frequency of your arguments and power struggles. This type of interaction minimizes conflict and promotes sharing and listening, so it allows each of you to learn new things about yourself and each other and makes your discussion more enjoyable. That means each negotiation makes the next Agreement to Negotiate easier because it leaves you with a positive feeling about the process and each other.

The skills demonstrated in the "agreement creating" conversation on page 93 are:

* How to give information that is easy to hear and understand about what you feel and what you want (*"I" Messages*).
* How to listen and play back what your partner said for confirmation that it's what was meant (*active listening*).
* How to make sure that the information received was what you intended to send (*attentive speaking*).

Learning these three skills can change your whole experience of talking from frustrating, volatile, argumentative, and futile (conflict-based) exercises into calm, satisfying, effective, and cooperative (agreement-based) discussions that accomplish what you intend.

Two of the skills that produce agreement creating discussions were popularized by Dr. Tom Gordon in *Parent Effectiveness Training*: "I messages" and "active listening." Both of these techniques, when used properly, help create an atmosphere of cooperation when the subject being discussed is difficult.

"I" Messages

Notice how the sentences that begin with "I" in the "Agreement Creating" column on page 93 are easy to hear. It is much less threatening to your partner when you say, "I feel hurt," or even "I feel angry," than if you say "You hurt me," or "You make me mad." When you acknowledge that your feelings are yours by saying "I," your partner is less likely to feel blamed and get defensive than if you begin with "you" (which focuses the responsibility on them) and more likely to be able to empathize and understand. By saying how you feel rather than blaming and accusing, you are much more likely to be understood.

"I" messages avoid the critical, attacking, defensiveness-creating atmosphere that "you" messages create. "You" messages consist of perceptions or judgments about the other person, usually couched in a critical, or even abusive, manner ("you didn't do that right," "you look terrible," "you made me so mad I wanted to hit you"). Of course, positive "you" messages (such as "you're beautiful," "you look great in that hat," "you did a great job," "you have a lovely smile") usually do not create problems, so it's only the negative, critical "you" messages we're talking about here.

Negative "you" messages are seldom useful in negotiating because they are upsetting and they will probably make your partner defensive, which prevents him or her from listening or understanding. Negative "you" messages are very difficult to hear because when we feel criticized and accused we naturally get defensive, focus on counterattacking, and stop listening to the other person. "I" statements, however, are easier to hear: "I feel defensive" is easier to hear than "You are attacking me." "I don't want to clean up the kitchen" is easier to hear than "You left a mess in the kitchen." "I" messages are the most effective way to make yourself understood to your partner because you are communicating information about yourself in a way that minimizes an argument. By using "I" messages, you express what *you* think, feel, see and hear without projecting your feelings onto your partner ("I'd like to go out with you more often" instead of "You never want to go out with me anymore").

"I" messages can be positive, too. ("I love you," "I feel great about the way we work together," "I am very satisfied with this decision"). Sharing information about yourself, your feelings, your ideas, and your reactions in this way helps your partner to understand you through your ideas and feelings. "I" messages can also be clearer and more direct: it works better to say, "I would like some time alone" instead of sighing and saying (passively), "Gee, it's so hard to get enough time alone" or (indirectly), "Don't you have to leave now?"

Exercise: Turning "You" Messages Into "I" Messages

The following exercise will help you develop your "I" messages skills, clarify what you want to say, and make it easier for you to be heard by your partner when you have a problem or a disagreement. You'll need a pencil and paper.

1. Review your relationship history and either:

a) Develop a list of "You" messages that created problems in the past, or

b) Observe yourself and your partner for a few days, and record on paper any "You" messages you hear.

2. Divide a piece of paper into two columns, as in the following example. *Write the "You" messages you collected in the left column and then practice turning each "You" message into an "I" message, as shown. Here are some examples to get you started.*

"You" Message	*Becomes "I" Message*
You never take out the trash.	*I want you to take out the trash as often as I do.*
You aren't home enough.	*I feel lonely and wonder if you still love me.*

You don't spend enough time with me anymore.	*I miss the time we used to have together and I'm worried that you don't care anymore.*
You don't pay your share of the bills.	*I want to renegotiate our financial agreement.*
Are you cheating on me?	*I feel insecure and suspicious because we're not having sex anymore.*

"You" messages communicate that you feel angry, frustrated, critical of your partner, or otherwise upset enough to say hurtful things, and they make getting agreement difficult. If your partner is defensive, or uncooperative, notice whether you are speaking in "You" messages. If you are, use the above exercise to change them into "I" messages and increase your chances of getting an agreement.

Active Listening

While "I" messages will help you speak more effectively, active listening can help you *hear* your partner better. When you ask for an Agreement to Negotiate, and your partner refuses, objects or avoids answering, active listening can help you understand *why* your partner is reluctant.

Once you know that, you can effectively reassure each other and create the agreement you want. Active listening means paying attention to your partner the way you'd like him or her to pay attention to what you say. To do this, you paraphrase (repeat in your own words) what your partner says to let your partner know that you are listening carefully, and to verify that you understood what your partner meant, as in the following guidelines.

Guidelines: Active Listening

1. Learn to recognize when your partner has something significant to discuss. *While some people have no problem saying, "I have something important to tell you," most of us usually* *aren't so clear. If you notice a change in your partner's emotional attitude or demeanor, (for example, you're normally talkative or cheerful partner becomes quiet, sullen or depressed, or snaps at you for no real reason, or is reluctant to discuss an issue or negotiate with you), he or she is probably troubled about something. Let your partner know that you care about his or her feelings and objections by gently asking for information about it: "Is there something you want to talk about?" or "Do you have a problem with what I said?" or "Is there a reason why you don't want to do this?" Ask, show your interest and caring, allow time for an answer, but don't push or insist.*

2. Do your best to pay attention to what your partner is saying. *You know you have succeeded in understanding what your partner means when you can repeat what you heard and your partner confirms it. For example, if your partner says, "You won't listen to what I want anyway," instead of arguing with that, just say, "You believe I won't care about what you want?". If your partner says that's what he or she meant, you have just reassured him or her that you're listening. If not, keep rephrasing what you heard (or asking your partner to repeat it) until your partner confirms that is what he or she meant.*

3. Ask questions if you don't understand. *If your partner is going on at length, you might say, "Could you stop a minute? I want to be sure I understand your last point before you go on to the next." Then repeat what you have heard so far, and get confirmation that you heard it the way your partner meant it. Don't allow yourself to become overwhelmed by a torrent of words or confusing statements; ask for explanations when you need them.*

4. Remember that listening to your partner does not necessarily mean you agree. *Even if you find that you still disagree, you'll have a better chance of solving the problem if you have a clear understanding of the opposing ideas. Saying "tell me more" is a wonderful way to be attentive to your partner when you are not sure you agree, but want to understand what is going* *on before you question or challenge your partner's statements. You may find that you simply misunderstood what your partner said at first, or that you're not as opposed to your partner's ideas as you thought.*

5. Take responsibility for speaking and listening. *If it seems to you that active listening means you have to take responsibility for* both *sides of the conversation, you're right, to a degree. Communication works best when both speaker and listener take responsibility for being heard and for hearing. While this may sound like a lot of work in the beginning, it will soon become obvious how much easier it is than arguing, fighting and not communicating.*

Here are some examples of "I" messages and active listening in action:

Michelle: ("I" message) *When you make a joke about a mistake I made, I feel hurt and criticized.*

Lou: (paraphrasing; active listening) *Do you feel put down when I joke about you?*

Michelle: *Yes, I do.* (confirmation)

Carol: ("I" message) *I feel like I do all the housework and all the caring around here alone.*

Joe: (paraphrasing; active listening) *Sounds as if you feel overworked and not cared about.* (asking for information) *Tell me more about that, I want to understand.*

Don: ("I" message) *I'm going to start riding my bike to work on Thursdays so I can save time getting to night class.*

Dale: (critical, negative response) *It's too dangerous. That's a terrible neighborhood and the traffic is fast and furious.*

Don: (active listening) *You're afraid I'll get hurt?*

Dale: (calmer, confirms) *Yes. It's too dangerous. I don't want you to get hurt.*

Don: (asking for Agreement to Negotiate) *I don't want you to be worried. Do you want to discuss the problem?*

Dale: (relieved) *Yes. I'd like to be part of your decision, too.*

Michelle: ("I" message) *Lou, I'm getting more and more uncomfortable about how we act with each other. I feel frustrated, unappreciated, and criticized.*

Lou: (defensive) *Well, why don't you talk back? Why don't you stand up for yourself? I'm not doing anything wrong.*

Michelle: (paraphrasing; active listening) *Do you think I'm accusing you of doing something wrong?*

Lou: (confirming) *It sure sounds like it.*

Michelle: ("I" message) *I don't want to accuse you, I care about you and our relationship. I see a problem that could get out of hand, and I'd like your help fixing it.* (asking for agreement) *Will you help me figure out what's wrong and what we both can do about it?*

Lou: (calmer, but still wary) *Well, when you put it that way, I guess I'll try.*

Sometimes, active listening makes it clear that someone doesn't quite understand, which gives you an opportunity to clarify it, as in the following interchange between Michelle and Lou:

Michelle: (hurt, using "I" messages) *When you made a joke about how I broke the blender last night, I felt embarrassed and incompetent. It's happened a lot and it's a serious problem for me.*

Lou: (confused, paraphrasing) *You're feeling bad because I comment on mistakes you make?*

Michelle: (explains more clearly) *Yes, but it's more the way you comment. When you make a joke, I feel like you're putting me down. It's an awful feeling.*

Lou: (catching on, paraphrasing again) *Being made fun of is the problem?*

> Michelle: (confirming) *Yes.*
>
> Lou: (offering to negotiate) *Now I understand. I didn't re-alize that my teasing upset you, and I wondered why you were so cold to me afterward. Do you want to see if we can sort it out?*
>
> Michelle: (agreeing to negotiate) *Yes, I'd like to get it cleared up. It's creating problems for us.*

Active listening allowed Michelle and Lou to get by a potential argument and clarify what was being said enough to reach an Agreement to Negotiate.

Attentive Speaking

The third component of Effective Communication is attentive speaking. Although a lot has been written, by Dr. Gordon and many others, about active listening, attentive speaking is less well-known and less understood, because it is a technique taught mostly to salespeople and public speakers to help them keep the attention of their customers or audiences, and to make them more aware of whether they're getting their ideas across (so they can convince more effectively, and thus sell more). It is a simple and highly effective technique that will help you communicate better with your partner, too.

Attentive speaking simply means paying attention, not only to what *you* are saying, but to how your partner is *receiving* it. If you watch carefully when you want to get a point across, your partner's facial expression, body movements, and posture all will provide clues (looking interested, fidgeting, looking bored, eyes wandering, attempting to interrupt, facial expressions of anger or confusion, or a blank, empty stare) to help you know whether you are being understood. By using the following guidelines, you can learn to observe your partner as he or she is listening to you, and see whether you are successfully communicating what you want your partner to hear, without any verbal communication from your partner. This is especially effective if your partner:

* Is not very talkative.
* Thinks disagreeing or objecting will "hurt your feelings."

* Is the unemotional, strong, silent type.
* Is easily overwhelmed in a discussion.
* Is passive, depressed, or withdrawn.

Sometimes, such partners are reluctant to let you know if they have a negative reaction to what you are saying. If your partner is not receiving what you are saying as you intended, and you persist in talking without finding out your partner's feelings, your partner could become more and more upset by what you are saying, stop listening, get very confused, mentally object or silently argue with you, or not want to be talked to at all. If you don't use attentive speaking to see the clues, you can be chattering blithely along, and suddenly your partner will react with anger, misunderstand you, or just lose interest in listening, and all your efforts to communicate are wasted. By using the guidelines that follow, you can figure out when you aren't communicating well or getting the reaction you want.

Using attentive speaking will help you:

* Avoid overwhelming your partner with too much information at once (because you will notice when he or she looks overwhelmed, bored, or distracted).
* Keep your partner's interest in what you have to say (by teaching you how to ask a question when you see your partner's attention slipping away).
* Understand when what you say is misunderstood (by observing facial expressions and noticing when they're different than what you expect).
* Gauge your partner's reaction when he or she doesn't say anything (by facial expressions, body language, and attentiveness).
* Tell when your partner is too distracted, stressed or upset to really hear what you're saying (by facial expressions, body language, and attentiveness).

Guidelines: Attentive Speaking

1. **Watch your listener.** *When it is important to you to communicate effectively, be careful not to get so engrossed in what you*

are saying that you forget to watch your partner. Keep your eyes on your partner's face and body, which will let your partner know you care if he or she hears you, increase your partner's tendency to make eye contact with you, and therefore, cause him or her to listen more carefully.

2. Look for clues *in your partner's facial expression (a smile, a frown, a glassy-eyed stare) body position (upright and alert, slumped and sullen, turned away from you and inattentive) and movements (leaning toward you, pulling away from you, fidgeting, restlessness). For example, if you say, "I love you" and you observe that your partner turns away and looks out the window, you are getting clues that you weren't received the way you wanted to be. Either your partner is too distracted to hear you, or he or she is having a problem with what you said.*

3. Ask, don't guess. *If you get a response that seems unusual or inappropriate to what you said (you think you're giving a compliment, and your partner looks confused, hurt, or angry; or you think you're stating objective facts and your partner looks like he or she disagrees; you're angry, but your partner is smiling), ask a gentle question. For example, "I thought I was giving you a compliment, but you look annoyed. Did I say something wrong?" or, "Gee, I thought you'd be happy to hear this but you look upset. Please tell me what you're thinking" or "I'm angry about what you just said, but you're smiling. Did I misunderstand you?" or just "Do you agree?"*

4. Don't talk too long. *If your listener becomes fidgety or looks off into space as you talk, either what you're saying is emotionally uncomfortable for your partner, the time is not good for talking (business pressures, stress, the ball game is on), your partner is bored, or you've been talking too long.*

If you think you've been talking too long or your partner is bored, invite your partner to comment: "What do you think?" or "Do you see it the same way?" or perhaps "Am I talking too much (or too fast)?" If you think it's a bad time, just ask: "You look distracted. Is this a good time to talk about this?" (If it is a bad time, then try again at a different time.)

5. Look for confusion. *When you're paying attention as you speak, incomprehension and confusion are also easy to spot. If your partner begins to have a blank or glassy-eyed look, or looks worried or confused, you may be putting out too many ideas all at once, or you may not be explaining your thoughts clearly enough. Again, ask a question: "Am I making sense to you?" "Am I going too fast?" or, "Do you have any questions?" Sometimes, just a pause in what you are saying will give your partner the room he or she needs to ask a question and get his or her confusion cleared up.*

6. Don't blame. *Blaming your listener—for example, by insisting that he or she just isn't paying enough attention—will only exacerbate the problem. Instead, ask a question, such as, "I don't think I'm explaining this clearly. Have I lost you?" or, "Am I bringing up too many things at once?" Phrasing the questions to show that you're looking for ways to improve your style and clarity invites cooperation and encourages teamwork.*

By using the above guidelines, you can find out immediately, as you are speaking, if you are communicating well with your partner. If you see signs of confusion or trouble, as Lou does in the following example, you can put things back on track quite easily.

After a busy period when Michelle and Lou haven't had much time for relaxation or with each other, they are in the kitchen getting breakfast before work:

Lou: *Hey, Michelle, I sure love you.*

Michelle: (Looks out the window and says nothing.)

Lou: (attentive speaking, asks for response) *Hello? Michelle, did you hear me? You looked away. Are you just tired, or is there a problem?*

Michelle: (angry) *I was thinking "talk is cheap" but I didn't want to say it.*

Lou: (active listening, paraphrase) *Do you mean that you don't believe that I love you?*

Michelle: (calmer, using mostly "I" messages) *Oh, I know you love me. It's just that I've felt neglected lately. You haven't been attentive, we haven't spent any time together, and I've missed it. Saying "I love you" isn't enough.*

Lou: (acknowledging, asking for negotiation) *You're right. We've been way too busy, and I miss you, too. Let's take some time off Saturday from chores and things, and sit down and discuss our schedule, so we can make more time for us.*

Michelle: (agrees to negotiate) *We do need to figure some things out, and it would be nice to talk. It's a date for Saturday.*

Lou's attentive speaking made him aware that Michelle didn't respond, and because of it, they were able to make an Agreement to Negotiate. "I" messages, active listening, and attentive speaking can improve your communication so much that you can usually overcome most of the barriers to getting an Agreement to Negotiate because your partner will feel cared about and listened to, and will not be as likely to get defensive, competitive, or argumentative. As you practice following the guidelines and become familiar with these Effective Communication skills, you'll find them very useful in all the steps of cooperative negotiation, in many of the exercises in the book, and even in your conversations with friends, family, and business associates.

Barriers to Agreeing to Negotiate

Even when you have good communication skills, you can fail to reach agreement because you encounter *barriers,* which are attitudes, beliefs, and old habit patterns that can make it difficult or impossible to move through the various steps to getting an Agreement to Negotiate. At these times, one or both of you will seem:

* Stubborn and unreasonable.
* Hopeless and depressed.
* Unable to communicate even though you've learned the necessary skills.
* So afraid or anxious that you cannot be reassured.
* Unable to stop arguing and begin problem-solving.

When these signs occur, you needn't panic or be discouraged. It simply means that you have encountered some of the barriers to agreeing to negotiate. You can learn to overcome each barrier. Once you develop the skills presented in this chapter, you will find getting to an Agreement to Negotiate with your partner much easier, even when the problem you are presenting is difficult.

The most common barriers people encounter in trying to get an Agreement to Negotiate are: *inexperience and mistrust, the power struggle habit, and the rescue.*

Trust, Inexperience, and Mistrust

If you are both new at Cooperative Problem Solving, neither of you will have enough experience at it to believe it is possible. As a result, you may have resistance to agreeing to negotiate. One or both of you may continue to argue, be too busy, agree and then not show up, or simply say no. The key to success is to allow yourselves to be beginners and learn the skills, and have extra patience with yourselves and each other as you try these new ideas.

In the first dialogue in this chapter, Michelle was able to state her problem, but forgot to ask for a negotiation. In the second example, she asked, but failed to notice that Lou had not agreed. However, after taking time to learn the skills of Gentle Persistence, clear communication, and Reassurance, Michelle could use these skills to enlist Lou in a negotiation:

> **Michelle:** (clear communication) *Lou, I'm getting more and more unhappy about how you talk down to me sometimes. I think we're both contributing to the problem, and I want us to sit down and see if we can sort it out and find a way of being together that feels better.*
>
> **Lou:** (shrugging her off) *That doesn't seem necessary, I'll just try to be nicer from now on.*
>
> **Michelle:** (gentle persistence) *That's not what I had in mind. We tried that Cooperative Problem Solving method before and I want to use it for this problem. It involves both of us and how we are together, so we need to agree to negotiate about it before we can go ahead.*

Lou: (resisting) *Seems like a lot to go through just because I criticize you sometimes. Why don't I just try to shape up a little and let's see how it goes.*

Michelle: (more persistence and clear communication) *Lou, this is important and I think we're both going to have to make a change or two, and it doesn't involve "being nicer." I want to agree on the changes we need to make, and I think you will want the same thing in order to resolve this. Will you reserve some time for negotiating this? I believe it will be worth it.*

Lou: (doubtful) *Sounds ominous. I don't know.*

Michelle: (reassuring) *I'm starting to feel like a nag, but I want you to understand that this is for us both. Remember that the purpose of negotiating is so that we both get what we want. We're not finished until we both feel good about the outcome. How about giving it a try?*

Lou: (reassured, agreeing) *You're very convincing. If you keep this up, I'll have to quit teasing you about not knowing anything. Okay, let's give it a shot. When do we start?*

When Lou has successfully negotiated a number of issues with Michelle, and seen that he gets what he wants, he will know from first-hand experience that the process works, and how to do it. With practice, you and your partner will learn where you are likely to get into difficulties and how to remedy them. As you find yourself succeeding more often, your confidence in Cooperative Problem Solving will grow, making it easy to agree to negotiate.

Meanwhile, there are skills (clear communication, Reassurance, and gentle persistence) that you can use to ease the way until you have your own backlog of successful negotiating experiences. We have provided sample dialogues throughout the book as examples to help you through your inexperienced phase.

Overcoming Inexperience and Mistrust

At the beginning, you may have difficulty getting your partner to agree to negotiate because one or both of you lacks the experience of success with Cooperative Problem Solving. Without an experience of success, cooperative negotiation can appear to be a lot of work with little or no benefit for the effort. If you are similar to Joe in the following dialogue, you like the way things are, and (like Carol) your partner wants a change, you might decline to negotiate.

> Carol: (stating problem, asking for negotiation) *Joe, I'm feeling burdened and overworked because I work and do all the housework, too. Will you help me figure out a way to cut my workload?*
>
> Joe: (resisting negotiation) *Any thing you come up with is okay with me as long as I don't have to do any housework. I'm much too tired for that.*
>
> Carol: (asks more clearly) *What I want is your help in solving the problem. It's a problem that affects us both and I want you to participate in coming up with a solution.*
>
> Joe: (refuses; shifts focus) *Well, I like the way things are, so it looks like only you have a problem.*

Because Joe and Carol are new at Cooperative Problem Solving, and Joe sees no benefit to himself in negotiating the problem with Carol, he's reluctant to begin. If your partner refuses to negotiate and you suspect that it is because one, or both, of you doesn't have enough experience with Cooperative Problem Solving, the Trouble Shooting Guide at the end of this chapter can help you figure out where the trouble is, correct the problem, and get on with your cooperative negotiation.

The Power Struggle Habit

For many couples, solving relationship problems has always meant a struggle where one partner may "win" the specific issue, but both of you end up unsatisfied and sometimes resentful. So it's not surprising if one or both of you would be unwilling to even try to negotiate for fear of reaching the same old outcome.

The struggle can be detected in the following patterns:

* *Guilt and Obligation:* This is the familiar "if you loved me, you'd ..." or "how can you do that to me (expect that of

me, not do that for me)" gambit. One partner uses guilt or obligation to coerce the other into doing something.

* *Threats and Emotional Blackmail:* This is the opposite of guilt. Rather than saying, "If you loved me..." the attitude here is "If you don't do what I want, I won't love you." In extreme cases, this can become very overbearing and abusive.

* *Courtroom Logic:* This is a relentless argument, lawyer-style, where one partner attempts to prove a "case," that they are "right," and deserve to get what they want. The argument sounds very logical, but it is completely one-sided and does not take the other partner's wants, feelings, and needs into account. In fact, it often belittles or "logically" dismisses them.

* *Keeping the Peace:* Passive partners try to be "nice" and give in to the above manipulations to "keep the peace" by never saying what they want for fear it will "upset" their partner.

* *Compromising: Both* partners give up *some* of what they want in order to reach agreement. It is time-honored as the "best" way to solve problems, but couples who do it usually find that resentment builds as they give up what they want bit by bit.

* *Hammering Away:* This is relentless persistence without gentleness or consideration for the other's wants, often called "nagging," "badgering," and "harassment." One partner just keeps insisting on getting what he or she wants until the other gives in.

A competitive, power-struggle approach to problem-solving is never pleasant for either partner. Even if the "winner" sometimes feels good about getting what he or she wants, there are unpleasant repercussions later when anger and resentment build up in the "losing" partner until it erupts in rage, depression, or separation. So, if problem-solving has meant struggles such as this in your history, it is quite easy to see why you or your partner might be hesitant to agree to begin the process.

When you ask for a negotiation, your partner might be suspicious that the offer is an attempt to manipulate him or her, especially if the two of you have a history of power struggles together. Dale, who is well aware that he and Don have a history of power struggles, reacts suspiciously to Don's offer to negotiate:

> **Don:** *I've been thinking about your idea of using the back bedroom for your office, and I'd like to use it for my office, too.*
>
> **Dale:** *But it isn't big enough for both of us. What's the matter with your office on Main Street?*
>
> **Don:** *I'd like to negotiate about this to see if we can both get what we want.*
>
> **Dale:** *Negotiate? I don't know what I would do for an office if you had the back bedroom. Why do you need to give up your office on Main?*
>
> **Don:** *If we negotiate, like in the book, maybe we can both be happy.*
>
> **Dale:** *Not if you get that room and I have to stay in the dining room.*
>
> **Don:** *Look, if I get the back bedroom, and that makes you unhappy, then we haven't done cooperative negotiation. Both of us have to be happy for the negotiation to be successful. Let's try it and see how it works.*
>
> **Dale:** *I can tell you right now, I won't be happy if you get that room and I don't. No way.*

In the above example, Dale is clearly refusing to negotiate. At other times, the refusal may not be so clear. Here is how Dale might refuse in an indirect or covert way.

> **Don:** *It looks like we both have our eyes on the back bedroom for an office. What do you say we try to find an answer?*
>
> **Dale:** *I'm busy, not right now, sorry.*
>
> Later.
>
> **Don:** *Want to talk about the back bedroom office situation?*
>
> **Dale:** *I've got a lot of work to do.*

Dale is not clearly saying he doesn't want to negotiate because he's not sure himself. He's feeling nervous about it, so he's just avoiding the subject in any way he can.

The guidelines and exercises in this chapter for overcoming the power struggle habit will show you how to overcome this natural resistance to struggling and replace it with confidence in mutual cooperation.

Reassurance and Overcoming the Power Struggle Habit

When you and your partner, like Don and Dale, are accustomed to power struggles, your Agreement to Negotiate can be blocked by the fear that the negotiation will be just another power struggle, someone is going to lose, someone will end up feeling bad, or nobody will win. Worse yet, after all the hassle, frustration, and resentment, the problem could still be unsolved. So, when you propose to negotiate, the response is "why bother?"

If you partner responds negatively to your request to negotiate, it may be because he or she fears the outcome of the negotiation. Determining the source of the fear (is it fear of losing? fear of arguing or fighting? fear it won't work?) gives you an idea about what is needed to reassure your partner.

Once you know how to reassure each other, as in the following step-by-step guideline, you will be able to proceed with making the Agreement to Negotiate. Reluctance or refusal to agree to problem-solving is usually the result of one or more specific fears, such as:

* Fear of being manipulated or overpowered.
* Fear of being taken advantage of, made a fool of, or "conned."
* Fear of having another fight.
* Fear that the process will be a long, complicated hassle (hard work) without a worthwhile result (a waste of time).
* Fear of losing, or having to give up something important.
* Fear that cooperative negotiation (because it's a new approach) won't go well or work at all.

FEAR	REASSURANCE
You're trying to manipulate me.	*I have in the past, but I've learned it doesn't work for either of us.*
You're conning me.	*I want to try this negotiation method and see if we both can really get what we want.*
You'll try to overpower me.	*The solution doesn't count if either of us doesn't like it.*
We'll just end up fighting and this will be another hassle.	*If we start arguing instead of negotiating, we'll stop and take a break.*
I'll have to give up something.	*If you don't like our solution it won't count—and you can even change your mind later.*
This is going to be hard work and a waste of time.	*It may be hard work because we have to learn how to do it, but if it works, it'll make our life a lot easier.*
I just don't trust this negotiation thing.	*Our solution doesn't count if we aren't both happy, so what can we lose by trying it?*

Each of these fears, and any others that might come up, can be discovered, communicated, and reassured. The following guidelines will show you how.

Guidelines for Reassurance

You'll need paper and a pencil.

Step 1. Find out what your partner's fears are. *If your partner won't agree to negotiate with you, and you suspect he or she may be afraid of a bad outcome or wishing to avoid a power struggle,* don't just assume you know that to be true. *You will be creating a secret expectation, which will confuse both of you, and increase your partner's resistance. Instead:*

A. Tell your partner what you observe that leads you to believe he or she is avoiding dealing with the problem ("We agreed to take turns taking out the garbage, and you haven't done your share," "When I ask you to negotiate, you say you're busy").

B. Because you are using "You" in Part A, be sure you let your partner know that you're just explaining what leads you to believe he or she doesn't want to negotiate, and ask your partner if what you see is correct, and if it does indeed mean he or she is reluctant to negotiate.

C. If your partner denies that he or she is reluctant, ask again if the two of you can negotiate, because there is no reason why not.

D. If your partner acknowledges (admits) that he or she is reluctant, let him or her know that you care about his or her feelings, and ask what the reluctance to negotiate is about. Whatever your partner says, don't argue about it. Listen to the answers carefully, and use active listening to find out the reason for the refusal.

If your partner has trouble figuring out what causes his or her reluctance, offer to read the list of fears on page 113 together to see what fits. If you acknowledge your own fears (as well as your partner's) as you read the list, you will maintain a cooperative atmosphere (and counteract the feeling that only one of you has, or is, a problem). To get fears into the open where they can be reassured, it is often helpful to consider what the worst possible outcome of agreeing to negotiate could be, and allow your imagination to run wild (What if you find out you're incompatible and you have to break up? What if you get into such a bad fight you don't talk for days?). If either of you are having such scary thoughts, it's better you get them into the open, where you can figure out how to handle those unlikely events if they do happen.

On the left-hand side of a piece of paper, make a list of the fears or fantasies that stop you and your partner from using cooperative negotiation. When your list is complete, you are ready to move on to Reassurance, in Step 2.

Here's how Don uses these guidelines (informally) in response to Dale.

Don: (offer to negotiate) *Will you work this home office problem out with me?*

Dale: (avoids issue) *Maybe later. I'm reading right now.*

Don: (lets Dale know what Don thinks is happening*)* *Dale, I've invited you several times to work this out, and I think you're avoiding it. Will you tell me why you keep putting me off?*

Dale: (begins to express fear) *I don't want to get into it. Why should I? If we talk about it, you'll just win the argument. I won't get anything I want.*

Don: (acknowledges fear by paraphrasing it, with active listening) *You think I'm going to try to talk you out of using the back bedroom?*

Dale: (relaxes a little, less defensive) *Yes. You've tried it before.*

Don: (more acknowledgment) *You're right, I guess I have overpowered you in discussions before. And now you're afraid I'm going to try it again?*

Dale: *Yes.*

Don is clear now that the problem is Dale's fear (from past experience) that Don will overpower him. Now, he can proceed to the next step and reassure Dale about what he has learned about the importance of both of them getting what they want.

Step 2: Reassure your partner. *Avoiding a power struggle is avoiding something unpleasant. If you can reassure your partner that the negotiation itself will not be unpleasant, and it won't lead to something unpleasant, he or she will have nothing to fear, and if your partner can be reassured that your negotiation can be a pleasant experience and the outcome can be very desirable, the resistance could turn to enthusiasm.*

In Step 1 of the Guidelines for Reassurance, you determined your partner's fears. Now, you can begin to reassure, by addressing each fear. To do that, consider each fear on the list and ask your partner what would reassure him or her and reduce the resistance. To reassure your partner, figure out together how you would handle the situation if his or her worst fears came true ("If the argument got so bad we weren't talking, we could see a counselor"). Knowing that you have a strategy to take care of yourselves if things don't go right will give your partner the additional confidence to try negotiation.

If any of the fears are based on things that have happened before, acknowledge that they did happen, and explain what is different now ("You're right, I did get angry and yell before, but I've realized that doesn't work, and I've learned to control my anger better"). On the list of fears from Step 1, write the solutions or reassurances for each fear, as in these examples.

When you have reassured each fear on the list, you are ready to go onto Step 3.

Once you get more accustomed to reassuring your partner, it can be done much more informally, as Don reassures Dale in the rest of their discussion:

Don: (more acknowledgment) *You're right, I guess I have overpowered you in discussions before. and now you're afraid I'm going to try it again?*

Dale: Yes.

Don: (acknowledging and reassuring Dale's fear) *I can understand how you'd think I was trying to argue you out of using that room, because I've done that before over different issues. I know I've used anger, silence, and shouting to win arguments before. But now I've learned some new things, and I realize that my old ways of winning have damaged the relationship. I want to try this cooperative negotiation where we would work together to come up with a solution we both like.*

Dale: (still afraid) *Yeah, but what if I don't like the solution?*

Don: (reassures again) *Then we keep working on it until we have a solution we both like.*

Dale: (not sure) *Sounds too good to be true.*

Don: (acknowledging, reassuring) *I know, but I think it's worth a try. We won't agree on anything that doesn't suit us both and if we can't do it, we'll be no worse off than we are now.*

Dale: (one last fear) *Are you setting me up?*

Don: (one more Reassurance) *No. I really want you to be happy with our solution. Will you give me a chance to show you, by trying a negotiation with me?*

Dale: (agrees, with reservations) *Okay, but if you yell or get mad, I'm quitting.*

Don: *Okay, it's a deal.*

Dale has been clear about his concerns and Don was able to respond directly, using the guidelines in an informal way. While Dale's agreement is not enthusiastic, it is a chance to try cooperative negotiation, and let the experience itself prove that it works.

Step 3. Ask for agreement to negotiate. *Once you and your partner are reassured that you will not fall into your old power struggle habit, the resistance to negotiating should subside. Now you can begin again by asking for an Agreement to Negotiate, and moving on into cooperative negotiation, as Don and Dale do here:*

Don: *I really want you to be happy with our solution. How can I reassure you?*

Dale: *Show me, I guess.*

Don: *Well, if we try negotiating, and I don't overpower you, will that show you?*

Dale: *Yeah, I guess so.*

Don: *Okay, let's negotiate this bedroom office problem.*

Dale: *I don't have to agree with your idea if I don't like it, and you won't get angry?*

Don: *No, because I want you to be happy, too. As long as you are willing to try to solve the problem with me, I won't try to push you into doing what I want.*

Dale: *In that case, I'm willing to try negotiating.*

At this point, Don and Dale have overcome the major part of Dale's fears about power struggles, and they can begin by working together to explore the Cooperative Problem Solving Process.

As you practice reassuring yourself and your partner, you'll find it gets easier to do, and the more Reassurance you give each other, the easier and smoother your negotiation will be. Reassurance will come up again and again throughout the book, because it can be useful when you are having trouble with any of the steps of negotiation.

The Rescue

If, as a result of having learned only a competitive approach to problem-solving and to each other, either you or your partner are accustomed to giving in, sacrificing, or compromising as a way to resolve conflicts, you may derail the negotiation process before it ever gets started by not letting your partner know what you want, or by giving in without negotiating, which we call a *rescue*.

There is an important difference in the motivation behind a rescue and the feelings that prompt an act of loving kindness or a gift. An act of kindness carries with it a sense of satisfaction and love. When you compromise in this spirit, you freely give a gift to your partner and it feels great. A rescue, however, carries with it a sense of oppression, irritation, sacrifice, power, superiority or inferiority (depending on whether you are the rescuer or the one being rescued).

You are rescuing when you:

* Give away all or part of what you want.
* Attempt to guess or anticipate your partner's wants, without considering your own.
* Try to please your partner regardless of what you want.
* Let your partner's real or imagined wants be more important to you than your own.
* Give in before problem-solving begins, as a way of avoiding painful power struggles.

People who view negotiation as a power struggle will frequently rescue to avoid a confrontation. They avoid Agreeing to Negotiate by doing the things listed above. A partner who rescues attempts to solve the problem by giving up all or part of what he or she wants, or by "mind reading," or trying to anticipate what a partner wants and give it before it's ever asked for. If you compromise, give in, or do a favor with a sense of sacrifice, resentment or superiority over your partner, then your action is a rescue. Cooperative Problem Solving requires both people to know and say exactly what they want, in order to achieve mutual satisfaction. You are rescuing, not cooperating, if either of you avoids problem-solving by giving up what you want. Letting the other person have their way may sound like "being nice," "cooperating," or "caring," but it leads to not getting what you want (with the resulting dissatisfaction and destructive resentment) instead of Cooperative Problem Solving.

Rescuing and being rescued are such common ways for couples to act in our society that it may sound like the way you "should" be in your relationship. Often the relationships we see around us (as well as those that are common in television, books, plays, movies, and songs) are built on rescuing and being rescued. Even though many people do it, and many think they (and you) "should" do it, rescuing and being rescued actually creates frustration, resentment, and dissatisfaction in relationships, and makes getting an Agreement to Negotiate impossible.

You cannot cooperatively negotiate with a partner who insists "There's no problem, we'll do it your way," or "I don't really want to do what I suggested, I'd rather do what you want." This is an attempt to be "nice," but it doesn't allow both of you to get what you want. If you propose to negotiate, and your partner just gives in, he or she is essentially saying no to negotiating. At these times, saying, "Okay, if you want to do it that way, it's okay with me," or "All right, I guess so" can be the equivalent of saying, "I would rather be dissatisfied than negotiate." You or your partner can do this once in a great while without creating a serious problem, but if it happens too often, it will leave the rescuer dissatisfied and resentful, eventually thinking "after all I've done for you..." or "if you loved me, you'd...."

When Carol tries to get an Agreement to Negotiate from Joe, he puts up a *rescue barrier*:

Carol: (frustrated) *I feel like I do all the housework and all the caring around here and there's no one to help me or even take up some of the housework slack. Will you help me sort this out and find a solution that works for both of us?*

Joe: (feeling overburdened at work, but not saying so, avoids the discussion at all costs) *Okay, okay, I'll do the housework this week.*

If Carol accepts this as a solution to the problem, Joe will probably be in a bad mood all week, do the housework be-grudgingly or poorly, and/or "forget" his promise, because he's rescuing to avoid problem-solving, and he has no real desire to help.

Another way to rescue is to not bring a problem up for negotiation at all.

For example, Fred might say to himself: "I'd join the Thursday night computer class, but it costs money and Naomi likes us to spend our evenings together, so I'll just forget it." Without Naomi's knowledge, Fred has rescued her. If he does this often, he'll eventually feel that Naomi is restricting his life and he never gets to do what he wants, and Naomi will wonder why he seems resentful.

Fred never told Naomi he'd like to take the class, or asked her what she felt. She might have welcomed the chance to have an evening to herself, to see friends, or to take some classes on her own. She may have been excited for him, and eager to support and encourage him. But if Fred never tells her, he will feel restless, restricted, and deprived. Neither of them will be fully aware that decisions have been made without discussion, and both will feel mystified and confused at their growing dissatisfaction with their Thursday evenings together.

You can even rescue your partner by having a one-sided conversation out loud, as Carol does here:

Carol: *I'm beat tonight and I don't feel like doing the dishes. Can we work a deal?*

Joe: (silence; he's reading the paper)

Carol: *You're probably tired, too.*

Joe: (still silent, oblivious)

Carol: *What if I just stack the dishes and if you don't feel like doing them, I'll wash them in the morning.*

Joe: *Okay.*

Carol has neatly argued herself into not asking for Joe's help in solving the problem about the dishes, and once again, has left herself solely responsible for the housework she resents. Joe is content, because he is getting what he wants for the moment, and he's unaware of Carol's resentment. However, he may well pay a price later for letting her rescue him because as Carol who is frustrated and angry, becomes grumpy, withholds sex, or gets angry over small things.

As we said earlier, agreeing with your partner without negotiating is not always a Rescue. Sometimes you truly agree with what your partner wants, so you are already getting what you want and a negotiation is unnecessary. If you feel satisfied, generous, and loving, and want your partner to get what he or she wants *and are not going to feel bad, resentful, or ripped off about it later,* you are giving and not rescuing. If it's genuine generosity, rather than a Rescue, the giver will feel good about it, not grudging or deprived.

The information and techniques in the following section, Overcoming the Rescue, will help you understand when agreeing is rescuing, and will teach you how to identify the related feelings and behaviors, how to stop rescuing or being rescued, and how to get an Agreement to Negotiate instead.

Overcoming the Rescue

If you feel dissatisfied with your relationship, or your partner seems resentful, and you are not able to discuss things with each other, rescuing is probably your problem. With this checklist, you can discover if you are a rescuer or if you are being rescued, and learn how to change these destructive patterns to achieve a greater degree of mutual satisfaction in your relationship. Following the checklist, you will find further exercises to help you overcome either problem.

Checklist: Rescue Discovery

Do you know if you are a rescuer? Or you are allowing yourself to be rescued? Check the statements that apply to you in the following checklist.

You Are A Rescuer If:

* You believe you must *do something for your partner that he or she* can *do for him- or herself, without being asked or giving them a chance to refuse.* "I hate cooking, but Dale would starve to death if I didn't cook a good meal every night."

* You do something that you do not want to do *for (or because of) your partner, and feel resentful later.* As in Carol and Joe's one-sided dialogue on page 120.

* You do not ask for what you want because you fear your partner's reaction to the request, you can't tolerate no for an answer, or you believe your partner is incapable of saying no. Fred is not asking Naomi about taking a class on Thursdays, page 120.

* You act as if your partner is incapable, treat him or her like a child, and act as a parent (giving unsolicited advice, giving orders, nagging, or criticizing).

* You do not tell your partner when something he or she does or says is a problem for you; and you don't ask for what you want your partner to do differently. Rose resents John's bringing business associates home on short notice; but doesn't say anything.

* You contribute more than 50 percent of the effort to any project or activity that is supposed to be mutual (including housework, earning income, making dates and social plans, initiating sex, carrying the conversations, giving comfort and support), without an agreement that your extra efforts will be specifically and adequately rewarded or compensated.

* You feel your role is to fix, protect, control, feel for, worry about, ignore the expressed wants of, or manipulate your partner.

Carol thinks she has to take care of Joe.

* You habitually feel tired, anxious, fearful, responsible, over-worked, and/or resentful in your relationship. Lou feels frequently overloaded.

* You focus more on your partner's feelings, problems, circumstances, performance, satisfaction or happiness than on your own. Rose is so concerned that John should be content that she allowed herself to slide into depression without noticing.

* You feel let down, ripped off, rejected, cheated, depressed, disappointed, or otherwise dissatisfied by your partner. Dale resents Don because he has allowed Don to overpower him in arguments.

The more of these statements you check off, the more likely you are to rescue, and the more you would benefit from the How to Stop Rescuing Exercise (page 125). The more familiar these feelings or actions are, the more frequently they occur, the stronger the habit you have of rescuing in your relationship.

You Are Being Rescued If:

* You believe you are not as capable, grown-up, or self-sufficient as your partner is. Michelle struggles to feel equal to Lou.

* You find that your partner is constantly doing things supposedly for you that you haven't requested or acknowledged (or may not even know about). Fred sacrificed the class he wanted "for Naomi." She was being rescued.

* You feel guilty because your partner frequently seems to work harder, do more, or want more than you do. Joe feels guilty that Carol works and does all the housework.

* You seldom need to ask for what you want, because your partner anticipates your needs, or you feel reluctant to ask because you know your partner will never refuse, even if he or she doesn't want to do it. Joe doesn't need to ask Carol, she does it anyway.

* You act or feel incapable, like a child: irresponsible, paralyzed, nagged, criticized, powerless, taken care of, or manipulated in your relationship. Michelle often feels like a child.

You act or feel demanding, greedy, selfish, out of control, over-emotional, lazy, worthless, pampered, spoiled, helpless, or hopeless in your relationship.

You contribute less than 50 percent of the effort to any project or activity that is supposed to be mutual (including housework, earning income, making dates and social plans, initiating sex, carrying the conversations, giving comfort and support). Without an agreement that your partner's extra efforts will be specifically and adequately rewarded or compensated.

You feel your role is to be fixed, protected, controlled, felt for, worried about, ignored, or manipulated by your partner.

You habitually feel guilty, numb, turned off, overwhelmed, irresponsible, overlooked, misunderstood, and/or hopeless in your relationship.

You focus more on your partner's approval, criticism, faults, anger, responsibility, and power than on your own opinion of yourself.

You feel used, manipulated, victimized, abused, oppressed, stifled, or limited by your partner.

Again, if you have checked one or more of the above statements, you are probably being rescued, and would benefit greatly from the How to Stop Being Rescued Exercise (page 125). The more familiar these feelings or actions are and the more frequently they occur, the bigger the habit you have of being rescued in your relationship.

Rescuing and being rescued seem "normal" because they are habits that were learned early in life and you have done for a long time. Such habits feel so natural it is difficult to be aware of them. Rescues are related to secret expectations (except they are your expectations of what *you should* do, instead of what your partner should do), and rescues also depend on secrecy. You cannot be rescued once you have given or denied permission, because you then have an open agreement, which can be negotiated, if necessary.

The following exercises are designed to help you learn to recognize a Rescue while you are doing it, making your unconscious behavior conscious. They will help you stop and think about what is happening and how you are rescuing so you can begin to change that behavior, and to change your Rescues into proposals to negotiate.

Exercise: How to Stop Rescuing and/or Being Rescued

The clarity you derive from doing this exercise will enable you to either avoid or correct rescue situations such as the ones in the Rescue Discovery Checklist, and is well worth the time and effort it takes to do it. Part 1 of each step will help you change your patterns of rescuing and Part 2 will help you change your patterns of being rescued.

Do the exercise when you are not *in the middle of a rescuing problem. Instead, reflect on your past experience and find the clues that will alert you to the next time you are tempted to rescue.*

Write down your answers. You may find it helpful to discuss these questions aloud with a friend or your partner.

Step 1. Recognize a Rescue while you are participating in it.

Part 1: *To remind yourself of what a Rescue is like, review the previous rescuer checklist. From your relationship history, choose a similar situation, and write a brief description of the events that were happening then. Answer the following questions in your description:*

A. What were the circumstances?

B. What were you doing (or not doing)?

C. What was your partner doing (or not doing)?

D. Was there a discussion? If so, what did you say (or not say); what did your partner say (or not say)?

E. If you had internal dialogue with yourself at the time, what was it about?

F. What was going on just before the rescue?

G. What led you to believe you needed to rescue your partner?

H. How did you feel about rescuing him or her?

I. What did the Rescue accomplish, if anything?

J. Now rewrite the scene and consider what you could have done, said, or perceived differently to correct the rescuing.

(For example, if you are rescuing, tell the other person what you're tempted to do or not do for them [how you want to rescue them] and ask them if they would like you to do that or not. Once you've offered and the offer has been accepted or rejected [even if your partner is not honest about what he or she wants, or makes a mistake] it is no longer a rescue. It is an open agreement, and can be renegotiated if necessary.)

Part 2: Review the Being Rescued Checklist in order to remind yourself what being rescued is like. Choose a similar scene from your relationship history. Write a description of the events that were happening then, and answer the following questions in your description.

A. What were the circumstances?

B. What were you doing (or not doing)?

C. What was your partner doing (or not doing)?

D. Was there a discussion? If so, what did you say (or not say); what did your partner say (or not say)?

E. If you had an internal dialogue at the time, what was it about?

F. What was going on just before the Rescue happened?

G. What led your partner to believe you needed to be rescued?

H. How did you feel about being rescued?

I. What was the result?

J. What could you have done, said, or perceived differently? (For example, if you are being rescued, tell the other person that you don't need him or her to do that for you, and suggest negotiating or talking about it. "Don, I know you think you have to cook dinner for me, but actually, I would like to get my own dinner sometimes, or even cook for you. Can we talk about it?" To remove the possibility of resentment without requiring your partner to change what he or she is doing, thank your partner and verify that it's truly okay with him or her, which will change the rescue to an open agreement.)

Redo the above exercises using several different scenes of rescuing or being rescued so that you can become as familiar as possible with the thoughts, actions, and feelings that indicate you are involved in one side or the other of a Rescue. *Once you can easily recognize a Rescue, you can move on to Step 2.*

Step 2. When you recognize that you are rescuing or being rescued, stop and think.

After doing the Rescue/Being Rescued Checklist and exercises in Step 1, you'll be much more aware of rescues in the course of your ordinary, everyday interaction with your partner. Once you recognize a Rescue, fixing it is quite simple.

Part 1: *When you notice the "cues" from the checklists in Step 1, stop in the middle of your interaction, and ask for a "time out," or a moment to think about whether you're rescuing or being rescued, and what the clues are. Tell your partner what you have observed, how you feel, and what you think happened. "I think I rescued you when I agreed to do all the yard maintenance last week because I feel resentful and I don't want to do it," or "I want to change my mind about agreeing to do the dishes every night. It doesn't feel fair to me."*

Part 2: *If you sense symptoms of rescuing, but you're vague about them or what they mean, take a moment to think about it, and review the following checklist:*

A. Are you putting out more or less than your share of the effort?

B. Are you reluctant to say what you want?

C. Are you wondering if your partner is honest about what he or she wants?

D. Do you feel uncomfortable about the interaction you and your partner are having?

E. Do you feel unsatisfied with the result?

F. Are you trying to keep your partner from being hurt, angry, upset, sad, or disappointed?

G. Does this feel similar to other interactions you've had, in which you wound up unhappy, dissatisfied, or hurt?

Yes answers to any these questions indicate a Rescue. If you answered no to all of these questions, you are probably not involved in a Rescue. If you answered two or more questions with a yes, proceed to Step 3.

Step 3. Propose to negotiate.

Explain to your partner that you feel uncomfortable with your interaction, and why. Ask if your partner is uncomfortable too. Often, you'll find your partner is as uncomfortable as you are. Discuss why you both feel resentful or unhappy, then ask your partner if he or she will negotiate with you.

In the dialogue from earlier in this section, Carol asked to negotiate new housecleaning arrangements and Joe volunteered to take over, even though he didn't want to. At first, Joe felt "noble" for helping Carol, but he soon realized he was feeling resentful, burdened, and that he was avoiding doing what he promised. Those feelings were his clue that he probably rescued Carol (Checklist and Step 1). He thought about the situation and realized that although he was fully understanding and supportive of Carol when it came to her feeling overworked and uncared for, he had a similar problem. He realized that he hadn't considered his own needs when he offered to do the housework (Step 2). At that point, he went to Carol and proposed to negotiate their housekeeping situation so that both of their needs could be met (Step 3).

You may want to give up rescuing or being rescued, but your partner may not. If you try the previous steps, and your partner still rescues, treat rescuing as a refusal to negotiate, and use the Trouble Shooting Guide (page 135) to overcome it. Remember: Even if your partner persists in rescuing or wanting to be rescued, if you state out loud what you believe is going on, you turn the Rescue into an open agreement, and open agreements can be discussed and negotiated.

Gentle Persistence

At times, no matter how good you are at communication techniques, how clearly you've Defined the Problem, or how carefully you've asked for an Agreement to Negotiate, your partner will still refuse. This can happen when you're brand new at negotiating, or even after you have had several successful, satisfying negotiations. Even experts can get stuck in refusing to negotiate, if they're anxious, stressed, or pressured.

There are a lot of possible reasons why your partner (or you) could be reluctant or unwilling to negotiate:

* If your partner has never heard of cooperative negotiating or is suspicious of the process.
* If the problem is particularly scary to either of you.
* If one of you is afraid of being manipulated or overpowered.
* If the problem seems insurmountable.
* If one of you is accustomed to being in charge.
* If the problem involves a life change.
* If one of you is in a stressful situation or anxious about something.

If you have tried all the techniques in this chapter and your partner still refuses to negotiate, don't give up! Cooperative Problem Solving and the resulting mutual satisfaction and success are worth some extra effort on your part. If you've tried everything you can think of, and your partner still won't agree to negotiate, *Gentle Persistence* is what you need.

Gentle Persistence is the art of staying focused on your objective (solving your problem, getting an Agreement to Negotiate) and repeatedly asking your partner to participate, *without sounding critical, impatient, pushy, overbearing, or dictatorial.* When it comes to getting an Agreement to Negotiate, Gentle Persistence can be a very effective and valuable skill.

Most of us only know how to persist in a nagging, complaining, whining, or angry way. These styles of persistence are based in the belief that the other person won't cooperate, and has to be made unhappy or uncomfortable enough to give in. Gentle Persistence, in contrast, is based on a belief that your partner is a reasonable person who wants to cooperate, but somehow (even after all your communicating, "I" messages, and invitations to negotiate) hasn't heard you, misinterprets or doesn't understand that's what you want. Here's how Rose used Gentle Persistence to get John to listen to her:

> Rose: *John, I want to talk to you.*
>
> John: (offhand) *Sure, go ahead—I've always got time to listen to the little woman.*
>
> Rose: (stating problem) *John, I want to get a job and I want both of us to work out a way for both of us to be comfortable with that.*
>
> John: (not believing) *Oh, Rose, you're not serious. What do you want, more money or new clothes?*
>
> Rose: (still calm, explains more) *No, John, I want to get a job. I want to get out of the house and meet people. I want to have a career. Can we discuss it?*
>
> John: (trying to distract her) *Now, now, Rose—why don't we just go out to dinner tonight?*
>
> Rose: (still calm, more definite) *John, please listen to me. I'm serious.*
>
> John: (looking for an excuse) *Is it your time of the month? You seem upset.*
>
> Rose: (still calm, firmer*) I am not having emotional, physical, or mental problems. I have made a decision about my life, and that involves you. I want your cooperation. I want you to know I am firm about this and I will keep bringing it up until you agree to discuss the matter with me like two adults.*
>
> John: (she got his attention with that, but he's skeptical) *Gee, I guess you are serious. But how can you mean it? Van Der Gelder women have never worked: my mother took pride in her house and children—she didn't need to work.*

Rose: (reassuring, still firm) *John, your mother was a fine woman. And so am I. These are different times. I want a new challenge. I know we can get your needs taken care of, too. A maid can keep house, and the children are grown. They don't need me. I need to feel productive again.*

John: (opening up, sharing fears) *But, Rose, what will my business associates think? What about our position? Who will take care of me?*

Rose: (reassuring, more Gentle Persistence) *I don't want to discomfort or embarrass you. Let's sit down and discuss it, and I'm sure we can work it out. We're both intelligent and creative. A solution that pleases both of us can't be too hard to find.*

John: (agrees) *Well, all right. I don't like it, but I'm willing to discuss it.*

Even though John is very reluctant to consider Rose's request seriously, her Gentle Persistence brought him around at least to a willingness to try. Such persistence may need to be repeated over a period of days or weeks if your partner is very reluctant to listen or has a difficult time understanding what you mean; but, if you can resist the impulse to nag or complain, it is very often successful.

When you gently persist, as Rose did:

* You let your partner know that the problem you're experiencing is very important and must be resolved, but in a gentle, uncritical, nonthreatening way.
* You gently but firmly refuse to give up your power to create good things in your life together, just because one of you is scared, angry, or stubborn.
* You stay focused on your purpose, and don't let yourself be drawn off course.
* You calmly and lovingly refuse to take no for an answer.

Gentle Persistence is not as hard as it may sound, and once you try it, you will be very motivated to do it, because it works. The reward for gently persisting is an Agreement to Negotiate, a mutually satisfactory solution, and a relationship that works for both of you.

Read and consider the following guidelines. If you become familiar with them, they will help you maintain your balance, and not be pushy and manipulative or give up too easily.

Guidelines: Gentle Persistence

1. Be well prepared before trying Gentle Persistence. *Gentle Persistence, especially when you're new at it, requires that you be in firm control of yourself. Choose a moment when you feel strong and you and your partner have some peaceful, uninterrupted time. You are demonstrating adult, thoughtful, calm, and rational interaction for your partner, even if your partner is aggravating, dismissive, or childish in his or her responses. So you must feel strong and comfortable enough to stay calm and positive in the face of negative responses. Be sure you're not upset, exhausted, fearful, or angry when you try it. That means you may need to take care of yourself by blowing off steam elsewhere (in writing, to a friend) if you get annoyed, or dropping the subject temporarily (and coming back later) because you've run out of patience.*

Understand that, until your partner realizes the importance of cooperative negotiation in general, or the importance of this particular issue to you, you are in the role of educator. Be sure you are clear that your goal is to get an agreement to negotiate about your problem and that you're willing to explain it as many times as necessary, remaining calm every time. Rose chose a time when she felt strong and calm and waited until she was clear enough (using the Problem Indicator Inventory, Chapter 2) about what she wanted to persist with John, and she successfully remained calm even when he seemed to belittle her.

2. You both deserve to have what you want. *Gentle Persistence is based on the conviction that you and your partner both deserve to get what you want. You're not asking for permission to have your way. You're making a firm offer to your partner to participate in the process so that he or she can have what they want also. If you hold that point of view, you won't feel guilty, helpless, hopeless, or angry. Remembering that you're working to create a change (from competing or rescuing to cooperation) that* *is beneficial to both of you and your relationship, and even raises the odds that your relationship will continue to be successful, will keep you objective and motivated to succeed.* Rose's conviction that she is doing something good and necessary for both of them shows in her statement: "John, I want to get a job and I want both of us to work out a way for both of us to be comfortable with that."

3. Be gentle and firm. *Gentleness means treating your partner with respect and caring, while firmness means not giving in or giving up. If your partner says something, listen and answer it (with Reassurance or "I" statements), but don't agree unless it's meeting your objective. Don't slide into nagging, manipulating, pushing, coercing, or abusing. Let your partner know that the issue is important to you, that you are serious about finding a satisfactory solution, that you want his or her participation in solving it, and you're not going to give up or forget the idea.* Rose used firm words: "I want" and "I've made a decision." She did not say, "Would you like to..." "I think I want..." "Maybe..." or "Would you be angry if I...."

4. Be sincere about cooperating. *Before you try Gentle Persistence, be sure that you really are willing to negotiate and that you honestly want your partner to be satisfied, too, so that your invitation to your partner to participate is genuine. If you really desire a cooperative, equal relationship, and your partner doesn't understand the value of that, it's up to you to lead the way. To succeed, you must accept the responsibility of being cooperative* whether or not *your partner agrees to participate.* No matter what attempts John made to put Rose off or distract or annoy her, she didn't lose sight of her objective, get angry, or disparage him.

5. Try to understand your partner's resistance. *Any or all of the barriers* (inexperience and mistrust, the power struggle habit, or rescuing) *can be in the way.* Use active listening *and* attentive speaking *to encourage your partner to talk about his or her reluctance, and review the sections in this chapter on the barri-*

ers. Rose used "I" messages frequently, and reassured John whenever he expressed a concern.

6. Be as objective as possible. *When you express what you feel, use "I" messages, and don't expect your partner to agree. Instead, try to see both sides: why you want to negotiate, as well as why your partner doesn't. The better you understand your partner's attitude and concerns, the more effective you will be at reassuring and convincing him or her that agreeing to negotiate will benefit him or her, too. Seek to explain the benefits of negotiating* as your partner would perceive them, *through Reassurance and active listening.* Rose's statements: "your mother was a fine woman," and "I know we can get your needs taken care of, too," were responses to hearing John's point of view.

7. Address your partner's fear. *You may need to reassure your partner many times while you are gently persisting, because you are changing the rules for how you deal with each other, and change is unsettling and produces anxiety. Unwillingness to negotiate almost always indicates fear of the outcome. It can be very reassuring to remind your partner, as Rose did: "I don't want to discomfort or embarrass you." Or our old standby: "I want both of us to be satisfied. I won't consider this negotiation successful or complete unless you get what you want, too."*

8. Remind your partner of your goodwill. *Love and respect usually reduce defensiveness and make cooperation easier. Take some time to remind yourself of all the good and valuable aspects of your relationship, and then share them with your partner. Tell your partner you believe that together, you can solve the problem. There is a further discussion of goodwill and how to establish it in the next chapter, "Setting the Stage."* Rose expressed her goodwill at the end: "I'm sure we can work it out. We're both intelligent and creative. A solution that pleases both of us can't be too hard to find."

With all the powerful techniques and guidelines you have learned about so far, chances are you will have gotten an Agreement to Negotiate by this time, and be ready to move on to the next step, "Setting the

Stage" (Chapter 7). But, in those rare cases where all the previous tech-niques have still not resulted in an Agreement to Negotiate, there are still some powerful remedies to try. The following Trouble Shooting Guide will help you figure out why your attempt to get an agreement didn't work, and tell you what to do about it.

Exercise: Troubleshooting Guide

This guide is intended to help you figure out what techniques to use if you've tried everything you can think of, but you're still "stuck" and cannot get an Agreement to Negotiate. The Trouble-shooting Guide will help you now, when inexperience is your problem, and also later, when you both have more experience with Cooperative Problem Solving, but you are unable to pro-ceed or figure out why. Returning to this guide will help you pinpoint how and why you are not getting an Agreement to Negotiate, and remind you of what to do about it. You will find this guide very valuable as a reminder of what techniques to use whenever you have trouble getting an Agreement to Negotiate (which is often the most difficult step of problem-solving), so keep it handy as a reference guide.

Use it the same way you'd use a troubleshooting manual for a piece of complicated machinery: look down the list of problems until you find yours, then read the instructions.

Problem 1: Your partner doesn't understand what Coopera-tive Problem Solving is, or doesn't trust that it will work. *Many of the concept and skills you will work with in negotiating will be new to both of you and if only one of you has read this book, the other may not know what is expected or intended. If your partner is interested in reading* How to Be a Couple and Still Be Free, *you can discuss it together. If not, you can explain cooperative negotiating in your own words, why it is important to you, and what about it is different from the way you usu-ally handle problems. (Use the skills of* Effective Communica-tion *page 92 and* Reassurance *page 112.) Once your partner understands what you are proposing and agrees that it is worth trying, you can show him or her the Negotiation Tree, and try again to Define the Problem and ask for an Agreement to Negotiate.*

Problem 2: You try to get an agreement to negotiate and end up arguing. *Did you ask for an Agreement to Negotiate in a way that your partner can understand? Find out if your partner has heard what you said and understands it. Make sure you are willing to listen to your partner's concerns as well as asking your partner to listen to yours. The more loving and respectful you are of your partner's feelings and opinions, the more likely it is that he or she will be open to and respectful of yours.*

Be sure you have used the clearest possible way to 1) give information about what you feel and what you want so that it can be heard by your partner, 2) make sure that your partner hears you as you intend to be heard, *and 3) verify, through listening and playing back what you hear, that you both understand each other.*

Problem 3: You believe your partner understands your intentions, but he or she still won't agree. *Your partner may not trust that cooperative negotiation can get you both what you want, and you may need to resolve these fears. Or your partner may believe he or she could be taken advantage of, or that you may waste your time trying to negotiate, or that you will end up in an argument, and damage your relationship. All of these reasons for not negotiating are based on fear. When your partner is afraid to cooperate, reassure him or her that you don't intend to harm, cheat, or degrade him or her by the process and that you care about your partner's feelings, wants, and needs, too. The essential attitude you need to establish in getting an Agreement to Negotiate is that* both *of you care about* both *of your wants, needs, and feelings. A negotiation is not cooperative unless* both *of you are satisfied with the result. Reminding yourself and your partner of this can make a lot of the anxiety and fear vanish and create an atmosphere where negotiation is much easier. The specific Reassurance to give will vary with the kind of fear being experienced. (Use the Guidelines for Reassurance, page 113).*

If you sense that your partner is worried, anxious, or afraid, ask what the fear is about: "Are you worried about something?" "You seem reluctant to work with me on this. Will you tell me why?" Once you understand what your partner fears, you can directly reassure him or her: "No, I'm not trying to talk you into something you don't want to do. I care about your feelings, too, and I also care about mine. I'm trying to find a way we can work to-gether so we can both *get what we want," or "No, we won't struggle about this all night. Let's try it for an hour, and if we haven't got it solved by then, we'll make a new date to try it again. We don't even have to do it right now. I'm just asking if you're willing to solve the problem with me. We can figure out a time to do it later." (See Overcoming The Power Struggle Habit, page 112)*

Problem 4: You've tried all the other suggestions and still can't agree to negotiate. *If you've followed Steps 1, 2, and 3 of this Troubleshooting Guide, and read through and applied everything in the chapter, and your partner is still unwilling,* don't give up. *Persistence is often the key to successful negotiation. Frequently, dropping the subject to give your partner time to think about it and then gently* bringing it up later *works very well. Especially if cooperative negotiating is new to you, your partner's initial resistance may be because he or she feels rushed or pushed, and needs some time to think about it before making an agreement. (See Gentle Persistence page 129)*

Problem 5: Even Gentle Persistence doesn't work. *When all else fails, the cooperative thing to do is to solve the problem your-self, inform your partner what your solution is, let him or her know you'd rather solve it together, and leave an open invitation for your partner to join you in cooperatively solving the problem at any time. Solving the problem to your own satisfaction, no matter what your partner may want, creates a great incentive for him or her to join you in negotiating, where his or her wants will be considered, too. The section on Solving it Yourself (page 139) will help you do this more effectively.*

Here's how Carol, using the Troubleshooting Guide, persuades Joe to learn about and try Cooperative Problem Solving:

Carol: (communicating clearly and inviting him to learn more about CPS) *Joe, I'm reading about Cooperative Problem Solving as a way of designing our relationship so it totally suits us both. It's about how couples can learn to work together better, so they both become more satisfied and happy being together. I'm really excited about it, and I'd like to try it out. Does it sound interesting to you?*

Joe: (not enthused, wary) *I don't know. What would I have to do?*

Carol: (offering options, reassuring) *Well, either you could read this book as I did, I could read it aloud, or I could explain it to you as I understand it.*

Joe: (more interested, still not sure) *Sounds interesting, but do we need it? Aren't we doing fine already?*

Carol: (communicating, persisting, reassuring) *I think there are things in this relationship that you would like and are not getting, and I think this is a way for you to get more of what you want, and to tell you the truth, there are a few important wrinkles for me that we need to iron out and I think this method sounds like it might help us do that.*

Joe: (cautiously considering it) *Okay, as long as you aren't expecting too much. I don't want to feel pressured to make a lot of changes because of some book, but I am willing to read it, if you give me a couple of weeks.*

Two weeks later.

Carol: (gently persisting) *Well, I know you read the book. What do you think?*

Joe: (still not convinced) *It sounds too good to be true, and also like a lot of work, and I don't know if it's worth it.*

Carol: (persisting, reassuring) *Joe, if it works, it'll be worth it, won't it? Remember my problem about housework? And I know you're not getting all the sexual contact you want. Maybe this will help us work those things out.*

Joe: (seeing some advantages to Cooperative Problem Solving) *I see what you mean, but it still sounds too good to be true.*

Carol: (persisting, saying she'll solve it for herself) *Let's try it just a couple of times, and if it won't work, maybe we'll try counseling or something else. I do think our problems aren't going to go away: they'll just get worse if we don't do something. If we don't try this, and you won't go to counseling, I'll have to go by myself, and work on it alone. You won't be participating, so you might not like the result. This, on the other hand, is focused on getting you what you want, too. Why not try it?*

Joe: (recognizing he could lose out if he doesn't try) *Okay, when you put it that way, I guess it's worth a try.*

When you obtain an Agreement to Negotiate, you are past the most difficult part of Cooperative Problem Solving. The next step in the Negotiation Tree, in the next chapter, is Setting the Stage, where you will learn to set up and maintain an atmosphere that keeps your negotiation in a relaxed, positive, non-confrontational attitude of cooperation.

Solve It Yourself

What do you do after you have tried everything and your partner still won't Agree to Negotiate? Up to this point you have learned many techniques for overcoming the barriers to agreeing to negotiate, and most of the time they will work for you. But what if your partner doesn't seem to care or acknowledge that you have a significant problem, or to be willing to help solve it? This section, solving it for yourself, will give you the information and guidelines you need.

Similar to many people, you may believe you have only two options if your partner won't agree to negotiate:

1. Either you can attempt to change the other person's attitude through force or coercion; that is, you can push, nag,

badger, pressure, whine, complain, reason, yell, resist, pout, or physically abuse your partner.

2. You can give up; that is, you can walk out, sacrifice, submit, comply, withdraw, withhold, or accept your partner's decision.

3. But there is a third option: You can choose to apply the steps of this guide to solve the problem by cooperating with or taking care of yourself. And when you have found a unilateral solution that solves the problem for you, you can reapproach your partner, stating your possible solution, and offering to renegotiate. We call this *solving the problem for yourself.*

If you are faced with a partner who won't, or can't, negotiate with you, solving the problem for yourself bypasses all the struggle, hassle and arguing, and goes straight to the central issue: solving the problem. This is probably the most powerful encouragement for your partner to join in and agree to negotiate, because he or she "loses a vote" and does not get to be part of the solution unless he or she works with you. This is not done in a spirit of "Okay, you won't negotiate, so I'll show you," but in a spirit of "I understand that you don't want discuss this, so I'll have to solve it for myself, as best I can. When you are ready to cooperate and negotiate, I'll be available."

There are several benefits to this approach:

* It is liberating to assert yourself on your own behalf and to realize that you don't have to have your partner's participation to be satisfied, yet not have to shut him or her out, or be unkind.

* You no longer have the problem you were concerned about.

* You can still have a good, loving, relationship, because you have not done anything bad to your partner (if he or she doesn't like your solution, he or she can negotiate), and you aren't feeling frustrated, angry, and deprived.

* It takes the pressure off your partner, and increases the likelihood that he or she will relax and be less defensive or more interested.

   *   It prevents you from being helpless and frustrated, so you are more able to welcome your partner's cooperation when he or she offers it.

The key to solving the problem for yourself is a belief that you are entitled to satisfaction. Caring about your partner's wants and needs (as well as your own) is central to cooperation, but you cannot effectively meet your partner's needs without his or her help. Therefore, when your partner refuses to negotiate, he or she leaves you no choice but to focus on your own need until he or she agrees to participate. As long as you offer every opportunity to cooperate and you extend an invitation to your partner to join you whenever he or she wishes, you are free to focus your attention on solving the problem for yourself. If you rescue and try to please your partner at your own expense, there is no chance for both of you to be satisfied.

The best solution is a course of action that puts you in control of your well-being; one that separates you from the effect of what your partner does or does not do.

Joe has stored up a lot of frustration, because Carol has been late too many times, so he's decided to try solving the problem for himself:

Joe: (angry, but calm) *I've been standing here waiting for you for 45 minutes. You said you'd be here at 6 p.m. Carol, this happens too much and it's not acceptable to me any more. I've tried to get you to talk about it with me, and you never want to.*

Carol: (sheepish, not too concerned) *I'm sorry. One thing led to another and I lost track of time.*

Joe: (determined) *I've heard that too many times before! I am not willing to be stood up like this again. It's too late tonight, the movie has already started, so let's go out for a bite to eat, and I'll tell you what I've decided about this.*

Carol: *Okay.*

At a coffee shop, a little later.

Joe: (persisting) *I said I'd tell you what I've decided about being late, so here it is.*

Carol: (trying to change subject) *Ah, Joe...*

Joe: (persisting) *No, please don't interrupt me. You'll want to hear this, because it will affect you.*

Carol: (agreeing to listen) *Okay.*

Joe: (firmly and clearly) *I don't want to be left waiting again. From now on, when we make plans, I will wait for 15 minutes, max. If you are not there in that time, I'll leave, so I don't have to get angry. If you call before our scheduled time and say you'll be late, and it's okay with me, we can negotiate about how long I'll wait. If we're going to a party or a show, I will leave a note and your ticket if any, and you can join me when you get there. But I don't want to miss any more opening numbers, or be late to any more movies, because I'm waiting for you. Also, I won't make plans to meet you anywhere where I will be embarrassed or uncomfortable if you're late, such as having to sit around a restaurant, wondering if you'll show up. Either we can go to the restaurant together, or we can invite someone else along, so I have someone to sit with if you are late. This way, I won't be angry, and we won't have to fight any more. On my part, I will be clear about when your being on time is important to me, and when timing is not so important, I will not be unreasonable about it. If I'm just puttering about at home, and you're late, that's really not a problem, and I won't turn it into one.*

Carol: (unhappy) *Gee, Joe, it sounds pretty strict.*

Joe: (standing firm, but explaining and reassuring) *It has to be, Carol, or I'll get so angry I won't see you any more, and there's too much that's good about this relationship to let a simple thing like this mess it up. I love you, but I just can't wait around anymore. It makes me feel unloved and uncared about, and that's not fair, because in many other ways, I know you love me.*

Carol: (resisting) *What if I don't agree?*

Joe: (offering to negotiate) *We can work out another solution together, one that makes both of us happy.*

Carol: (thinking about it) *Maybe that's a good idea. Let's make a time to discuss it.*

Sometimes, problems are more serious, and solving it yourself is necessary to protect yourself, as it is with Carla and Ann. In the following example, Carla is frustrated about the way her partner, Ann, deals with money, to the point that Carla's credit and financial security are being jeopardized—an issue that creates problems for many couples.

Carla: (concerned) *You haven't been contributing to our household account lately. You already owe me money from the past, and for three weeks, I've bought the groceries and paid this month's gas and water bills. Are you in financial trouble again?*

Ann: (offhand) *I've had some expenses. I'll get caught up on payday.*

Carla: (not accepting that answer, persisting) *Your half of the current expenses so far is $185 and I'll need money for next month in the account, which is another $200 plus the rent.*

Ann: (still unconcerned) *Okay.*

After payday.

Carla: (persisting) *Do you have the money for the household account?*

Ann: (casual) *I'm a little short. Here's $100 and I'll catch up on the rest later.*

Carla: (not going along) *I'm feeling used here. I want you to pay your share and you're not. I want to talk this out and get this problem solved.*

Ann: (denying) *Look, there's no problem. I'll be all caught up next week.*

Carla: (persisting) *Ann, I've heard that before. I have a problem with how we handle money together, and I want to work it out with you.*

Ann: (getting defensive) *I told you not to worry about it. I'll take care of it next week. Now, leave me alone.*

Carla: (realizing she's not getting cooperation, asking for negotiation) *You don't seem to understand that I'm feeling really bad about this. I love you a lot and I'm worried about our relationship. How can we be together if you're not paying for your half? I don't earn enough for both of us, and even if I did, it isn't fair. Let's sit down tonight and work this out. This is very serious.*

Ann: (refusing, changing subject) *Will you please just relax. Let's go out and lighten up. I'll treat for a movie tonight.*

Later, after pondering the whole situation, Carla decides it's serious enough that she has to solve it for herself. She decides to resort to a tough solution. In the midst of her emotional turmoil, Carla doesn't trust herself to be clear and calm in conversation with Ann, nor did she think Ann would take her seriously unless she wrote it down, so Carla writes the following letter, which is a good way to be sure Ann has a chance to understand Carla's unilateral decision:

Dear Ann:

As you probably realize, I am very unhappy with our current financial dealings. I don't seem to be able to find a way to get you to see how important it is to me that you pay your share of expenses, on time, and without being reminded. I've attempted to discuss this with you, with no success. So, I've made a decision on my own. I've thought this through very carefully, and I want you to know how very much I love you. I am very sad and frustrated because I can't find a way to encourage you to help me reach a solution that will work for both of us.

I've decided to solve the problem as best I can without you and here's my solution.

* I'm only going to buy food for myself. I won't share it with you until we work the problem out.

* You have a good job, and you make enough money to live on. I don't know what's wrong, because you won't tell me, but your lateness on bills and the rent is beginning to ruin

my credit, and I'm no longer going to pay your share. I'm giving you 30 days' notice that if you don't pay your share of the expenses and the rent, we'll use the last month's rent we have coming next month, and I'll move out. I hate doing this, because I like living with you, but it seems like the only way to protect myself from your money problems.

* If that happens, I would still like to see you, and be your partner, but without the financial entanglements. I want us both to be happy and be able to stay together, so if you want to work this out some other way, and pay your full share, or at least tell me the truth about what's wrong, I'm more than willing to help. If you have a suggestion about how you can get what you want and I can still feel financially secure, I'd be happy to discuss it, but I can't accept any more empty promises. I just am not willing to feel used and taken advantage of any more. It's damaging my feelings for you.

With much love and some anger,

Carla

In the above letter, Carla has taken a stand on behalf of herself, and what she believes is her only chance for a satisfying life with Ann. Carla's solution is drastic, but very effective at releasing her from the problem Ann is causing. She knows that if this money issue goes on any longer, her good feelings about Ann will be destroyed, and so will their relationship. In this way, Carla has regained control of her financial well-being, and still left an open invitation to Ann to continue the rest of the relationship, and even to renegotiate their financial arrangement on a more honest and realistic basis. Ann still has choices, but she no longer can put Carla in financial jeopardy.

Ann has a good job, and makes enough money to support herself, so her nonpayment is evidence of a serious problem that requires a strong, tough solution. Even though Carla is horrified at the thought of losing Ann, she isn't willing to sacrifice herself and allow Ann's financial problem (and Carla's own anger) to get worse.

This letter has an excellent chance of getting Ann's attention and achieving Carla's true goal, which is to work together on the problem. If Ann still won't negotiate, then her problem is severe, and Carla truly needs to protect herself by separating her funds from Ann's. At this point, Carla must allow Ann to make up her mind about what she wants to do. By putting their relationship on the line, while also continuing to offer to negotiate, Carla is presenting the strongest possible motivation for Ann to want to deal with the problem, and also protecting herself in case Ann is so out of control that she can't fix it.

If your problem is not as serious as Ann and Carla's, then your solution will be much less drastic, similar to Joe's, but the attitude of taking care of yourself while leaving the offer to negotiate open is the same.

In solving this serious problem for themselves, Carla and Joe followed several steps. By following the same steps, you can be sure you've given your partner ample opportunity to cooperate, and you're not overreacting.

Guidelines For Solving It Yourself

1. Be sure you've made a thorough attempt to negotiate. *Have you Defined and Communicated Your Problem, using all the techniques in Chapter 2* (problem inventory, creating permission, analyzing rights and responsibilities, and discovering secret expectations)? *Have you used all the techniques and skills in this chapter in asking for an Agreement to Negotiate* (overcoming inexperience and mistrust, communicating clearly, Reassurance, and Gentle Persistence)? *To cover these steps, Carla opens her letter with a review of the problem and statements that she's tried to negotiate it. Review the problem and your attempts to solve it before telling your partner that you're solving it yourself. You can then open your discussion or letter as Carla or Joe did.*

2. Tell your partner what you are doing. *State clearly that you have attempted to negotiate the problem, that your assessment is that your partner doesn't want to work on it, that you would prefer to work on it together, but that you've decided what you are going to do about it on your own. Carla writes how* *sad she is to have to resort to such a stern solution, Joe explains that he's protecting what's good about the relationship.*

3. Invite your partner to negotiate at any time. *Say, as Carla and Joe did, that you are going to follow your own solution unless your partner wants to discuss it, but that you are open to discussing it at any time if it makes him or her unhappy. This is your open invitation to negotiate at any time. It is important because it keeps the attitude of cooperation intact. Without the open invitation, Solving It Yourself can become a power play.*

4. Communicate your goodwill. *Let your partner know that you value him or her and the partnership, and you don't like having to make unilateral decisions, but you feel you have no choice, because you can't force him or her to work on it with you. Carla said how much she loved Ann, and how she hated to do this, and Joe says he wants to protect his good feelings for Carol.*

5. Be sure your solution solves the problem for you. *Using the Stating Wants and Exploring Options exercises in Chapters 5 and 6, find a solution that solves the problem in a way that's satisfying for you, even if you think your partner may not like it. If the solution works for both of you, the problem is solved, and needs no further discussion. If your partner is not satisfied with your solution, he or she has already been invited to negotiate, and being left out is a powerful incentive.*

A good rule of thumb in finding your own solution is to imagine what you would do about the problem if your partner weren't part of it. What would you do if your best friend was involved? Would it be different? Would the problem change if you lived alone or were single? What would you do then? Considering a relationship problem from the vantage point of a single person often points out places where you're being needlessly dependent.

Because she was in financial jeopardy through her partner's refusal to cooperate, Carla's solution had to be financial untangling from Ann, while hoping to retain the emotional connection. If Ann does genuinely care, and is not just using Carla for financial support, this decision will get her attention, and get her interested in solving the problem. If not, Carla is at least saving herself from a disastrous financial situation. Before Carla made the decision, Ann's irresponsible behavior was Carla's problem. Now it has become Ann's problem. Joe's problem is less severe because it is just an inconvenience, but it still adversely affected his feelings for Carol. Joe's solution eliminates his feeling of powerlessness and not being cared about, and allows Carol's problem with lateness to affect only her.

In obtaining an Agreement to Negotiate, you have learned to communicate what you want; how problem-solving works; to reassure and encourage your partner to participate; to persist gently, until your partner understands how important it is to you; to overcome inexperience and mistrust by using the Troubleshooting Guidelines; turn power struggles into cooperation; change old habits of rescuing and resenting the result; and, if all else fails, to solve the problem yourself in order to demonstrate that problems can be solved and motivate your partner to be part of your solution.

Hopefully, you will seldom need to solve a problem without your partner's cooperation, but knowing you can solve the problem for yourself and still leave the door open to your partner's participation means you can remain calm and gentle in the face of a partner's reluctance to cooperate.

This will certainly be better for your relationship than feeling frustrated, angry, and taken advantage of. These skills create an atmosphere of cooperation between people, and lead to negotiation that satisfies everyone involved. In the next chapter, you will learn the next step of Cooperative Problem Solving after you do have an Agreement to Negotiate: Setting the Stage.

Chapter 4

 Set the Stage

In the last two chapters, you learned to Define and Communicate Your Problem and Agree to Negotiate. These are often the most difficult steps of the Negotiation Tree, because they are the entrance to a system of Cooperative Problem Solving that conflicts with the competitive attitudes and beliefs most of us are taught; they contradict the "win or lose" beliefs many of us have about relationship problem-solving. Once you've accomplished those two steps, you are well on your way to a Free Couple Relationship, teamwork and cooperation in your negotiation. The next step, Setting the Stage, means creating an atmosphere and attitude conducive to cooperation and, therefore, to successful problem-solving. Setting the Stage has four parts: *choosing time and place, establishing goodwill, reassurance, and setting aside held hurt and anger.* Taking the time to do these four procedures helps you create an environment that will greatly enhance and ease your negotiation, and make reaching a cooperative, mutually satisfactory decision much easier.

Setting the Stage is designed to make solving your problem as easy and efficient as possible, because by doing it, you create the proper environment for effective Cooperative Problem Solving and further establish a mutual feeling of cooperation and teamwork by making sure you are both comfortable and available for uninterrupted discussion.

While it takes a whole chapter to fully explain and to teach you the skills you need, you'll find that in actual practice, Setting the Stage usually takes only moments.

Setting the Stage consists of four parts:

1. *Choose the time and place for negotiating.* Having enough uninterrupted time to negotiate in a calm and relaxed manner, as well as a time both of you have agreed on, gives your Cooperative Problem Solving a better chance of success than trying to rush through it before running off to work, too late at night, or in between talking to children or answering phone calls.

2. *Establish goodwill.* Sharing your positive intent about your relationship, and your good history together, reminds you of the positive aspects of your relationship at a time when you may feel stressed and focused on a problem. This mutual feeling of goodwill allows you to negotiate in a positive atmosphere, increases your motivation, and reminds you that you have an investment in each other that is worth working on.

3. *Reassure each other.* Reassurance calms you down when you're anxious about the result of the negotiation, and reminds you that this negotiation is only about a single problem, and does not mean your whole relationship is in jeopardy.

4. *Set aside held anger and hurt.* Often, when problems are not solved right away, couples store frustration and disappointment until they feel so angry and hurt they cannot negotiate calmly and rationally. You can learn to set aside accumulated hurt and anger so your feelings will not interfere with your communication and cooperation.

Choosing Time and Place

Couples who do not set the stage properly, even though they've defined the problem and agreed to negotiate, can wind up feeling harried, confused, angry, and/or trapped in negotiating when they don't have the time, the energy, or the goodwill (motivation) to carry on. The resulting tension, if allowed to build, can sidetrack the negotiation into conflict and impede all the progress you've made in defining the problem and agreeing to negotiate, especially if you and your partner are new to Cooperative Problem Solving or are negotiating a particularly difficult or long-standing problem.

Too often, couples who realize there is a problem may agree to solve it together, but they pick a time when they feel rushed or tired, or pick a setting that is uncomfortable, not private enough, or has too many interruptions, or, they are too vague about where and when, and the discussion doesn't happen. The bigger and more long-standing the problem is, the more important setting a time and place becomes.

Poor conditions work against successful negotiation because they make it difficult to stay focused and think clearly. If lack of time, tiredness, or a harried, anxious atmosphere interferes with your cooperation and problem-solving, you can become discouraged and afraid that your negotiation won't work. Choosing a time when you both are rested and relaxed, in which you won't be rushed or interrupted, stacks the odds in favor of successful negotiating. It allows you the time you need to think clearly and to explore, in a relaxed setting, all the aspects of the problem you are negotiating. Uninterrupted time will allow you to complete your negotiation as quickly and efficiently as possible, and reduce tension between you. Properly setting the stage not only makes sure you have enough time and a good setting for uninterrupted negotiating, it also helps you establish the emotional climate of mutual caring and teamwork that is essential to Cooperative Problem Solving. Without it, you are more likely to see each other as competitors and will be unable to work together cooperatively.

Rose, after figuring out how to Define the Problem, and getting John's Agreement to Negotiate, agrees to put off the discussion until "later," because John has work he brought home from the office. Days pass, and nothing more is said. Rose, who struggled to bring up the problem in the first place, feels reluctant to broach the subject again, but she finally does.

Rose: (hesitantly) *John, do you remember when I said I had a problem about the children being gone and not having enough to do?*

John: (reading papers) *Uh-huh.*

Rose: (without much hope) *You said you'd discuss it with me.*

John: (distracted) *Not now, dear, I'm tired.*

Rose: (disappointed) *Okay.* (gives up)

Now getting angry, Rose tries again the next morning.

Rose: (quietly fuming) *John, you said you'd discuss the problem with me, and I want to talk about it now.*

John: (rushed) *Rose, don't pester me before work. You know I have to catch my train. I don't have time now.*

Rose: (angry) *Work, work, work! It's all you ever think about. You never want to talk about my important issues. You love your work more than you love me.*

John: (angry, too) *Okay, I've had it! Don't you dare complain about my work. I've earned a good living for you and the children all these years. Just leave me alone.* (grabs coat and briefcase; leaves and slams the door.)

Rose and John have just wiped out all the progress they made on the first two steps, and now they're both angry. Why? Because neither of them realized how important choosing a time and place was. Rose picked a time when John was tired, and he didn't realize that she was trying to reopen the negotiation. Then, because she was frustrated at his lack of response, she became impatient and anxious, and tried to insist on negotiating at a time when John had to catch a train. He felt badgered and trapped, and responded by getting angry and leaving. They had an Agreement to Negotiate, but they had neglected the first step to Setting the Stage: choosing a time and place agreeable to both of them.

Later, once they learn to use this step of the Negotiation Tree, they are more thoughtful about when and where they negotiate.

Rose: *John, do you remember when I said I had a problem about the children being gone and not having enough to do?*

John: (reading the paper) *Uh-huh.* (Puts down paper, thinks a minute) *Oh, yes. We agreed to negotiate. When do you want to do it?*

Rose: (considering time and place) *I know you're tired now, and it wouldn't go very well. What about having a nice dinner at home tomorrow night, and then sitting down to talk afterward?*

John: *That sounds good.* (agrees on time and place) *I'll make sure I'm home by 6. Will that work?*

Rose: (agrees) *Thank you. I really appreciate your cooperation. I'll make your favorite dinner, and then we can talk.*

John: (satisfied) *It will be a pleasure. We need a good, long talk and some time together.* (goes back to his paper. Rose, reassured, picks up a book)

What Rose and John have done is to Choose the Time and Place of their negotiation.

The following steps will help you choose a time and place effectively.

Exercise: Choosing Time and Place

1. Evaluate the problem for time needed. *Consider the problem you are negotiating.*

* Has it been long-standing?

* Does it seem that you are on opposite sides and will never agree?

* Are you able to think of several possible solutions, or are you locked into just one outcome?

The more difficult the problem seems, and the more insistent either of you is on a certain outcome, the longer it will probably take to solve the problem. The more relaxed you are, and the more open-ended time you have, the more likely it is that the problem will be easily solved. So, if the problem seems difficult, choose a time and place that is open-ended, or decide in advance that the negotiation may take more than one session. When you're new at Cooperative Problem Solving, allow more time than you think you need. As you become more familiar with the process your estimates of time needed will become more accurate.

2. Consider both your schedules. *Many couples have different schedules and preferences. One of you may be a "morning person," more alert and better-natured in the morning, and the other a "night person," more apt to be effective in the evening. Both of you may be busier on weekends (with kids, laundry, shopping, etc.) and more relaxed on weeknights after work. Or perhaps your work schedules conflict. Compare your schedules, and select a time that works well for both of you.*

If one of you is more stressed about the problem, choose a time that makes it easiest for that partner. Experiment, and after trying a few negotiation sessions at different times, you'll find the best times for problem-solving.

3. Arrange to be uninterrupted. *When choosing time and place, remember that it is important to be uninterrupted. Turn on the answering machine or take the phone off the hook; find a way to occupy the children, or see if a relative or neighbor will watch them for a while; and don't answer the door.*

Establishing Goodwill

In a couple relationship, goodwill is a combination of the trust, affection, and positive regard the partners have toward each other. People who like and respect each other get along better because they feel cared about, appreciated, trusted, and caring toward each other. When you and your partner establish the goodwill you have for each other while you are cooperatively problem-solving, you will have an easier time working together to solve the problem because you will be reminded that solving this problem is a way to enhance the good relationship you already have.

Establishing goodwill reminds you that you are working together to solve the problem, rather than struggling with each other; it helps you to remember that you both desire *mutual* benefit and satisfaction; and increases your pleasure in accomplishing something together.

Partners who try negotiating without establishing goodwill can forget to put the problem in its proper perspective to the relationship, see their partner as an "enemy" (competitor), and regard fixing the problem as *their only chance* to make the relationship work. If that happens, in their anxiety they may compete, fear being taken advantage of, or fear that the negotiation will degenerate into an argument.

> Rose and John, before they learned to establish goodwill, had many heated and frustrating encounters such as the following:
>
> After dinner, at the agreed upon time.
>
> Rose: (abruptly, anxious, not clear) *Okay, John, let's discuss my problem. I'm unhappy, and I feel restless and useless. I can't go on like this.*
>
> John: (getting tense) *What do you want to do?*
>
> Rose: (not problem-solving, just reacting) *I don't know. I just feel unhappy. Maybe I should get a job.*
>
> John: (back to his old ideas) *Rose, you don't need to work. I make enough money. I want you here at home.*
>
> Rose: (angry) *You just don't hear me. I have to do something meaningful.*
>
> John: (angry) *So find something meaningful to do! Don't bother me with it!* (discussion ends with both of them dissatisfied and frustrated)

After Rose and John learn the importance of establishing goodwill, the dialogue goes differently:

> Rose: (talks about good feelings) *John, I appreciate you being here to discuss this problem with me. You and I have solved a lot of problems together, and I trust your advice and judgment.*
>
> John: (lets her know he cares) *Rose, I enjoyed this meal, and I'm looking forward to our discussion. You know that I have always wanted you to be happy, and I'm sure we can work this out together.* (Both are now reminded of their long, successful association, and are ready to work together to solve the problem, which now feels more mutual.)

If, when you attempt to Set the Stage, you find that warmth and good feelings are not flowing between you and your partner, the following exercise can help you learn to express and develop your loving appreciation for yourselves, each other, and your relationship. This exercise will help you draw on your relationship history to establish goodwill, so that you and your partner can remember that you're an experienced team with a history of successful and positive interaction. Negotiations are bound to go better when they begin in a calm, positive, and hopeful atmosphere.

Exercise: Establishing Goodwill

You'll find that the few moments it takes to establish goodwill, as in this exercise, will make problem-solving vastly easier by reminding and reassuring both of you that you are partners, that you have had some successes together, and you genuinely want to work together to solve this problem and to build a better relationship. We recommend you always establish goodwill after choosing time and place, and before the rest of the negotiation, and you can also use it any time the atmosphere gets tense, or you get discouraged or worried about the outcome of your negotiation.

Step 1. Review past successes. *You and your partner, like every couple, have had successes, even if they seem hard to remember when you are struggling. Your courtship was a success, or you wouldn't be together. You have had good times together and accomplished some goals together. Perhaps you have had children; bought a house or a car; saved some money; gone to a movie or dinner; celebrated anniversaries; survived illnesses; furnished your house or apartment, renovated, painted and/or cleaned it up together; visited family or friends; taken vacations or trips together; and spent weekends, days off or holidays together. A good way to begin to Establish Goodwill is to remind each other of these good times. You will not only reactivate your loving feelings, but you will be reminded of what is possible between you and why you are together today.*

If you find yourself slipping into feelings of regret, hurt, or anger because you don't experience those good times as much lately, see if you can return your attention to the good times and the loving feelings and go on to Part A. If you can't, go to the section Setting Aside Held Anger and Hurt on page 163.

Part A. Select Three Positive Events. *Select three of the positive events or successful interactions from your history, where you felt good about your partner, and were enjoying the relationship. Go back in time as far as you need to in order to find the good feelings (to the first excitement of meeting each other and dating, if necessary). Think about your three positive events for a few minutes, and remember them clearly enough to describe them to your partner, and write them down, if you wish, before going to Part B.*

Part B. Share Positive Memories. *Now, take a few moments to share the memories you have collected, to remind yourselves and each other how good things can be. Discuss your positive memories quietly and gently, until you feel some of those positive feelings toward each other right now. Whatever tension this problem has caused between you should relax as you share your positive memories and remind yourself that you're a partnership. When you feel a sense of connection and partnership, go on to the next step. (If you get stuck here, and can't reach your good feelings, use the Setting Aside Held Anger and Hurt Exercise, page 165, and then return to this exercise.)*

Step 2. Acknowledge the importance of your partnership.

Neither of you would even be trying to resolve the issues between you if your partnership wasn't important to you. Remind each other that you care about the relationship, and about yourselves and each other. You have made an investment of time, energy, and caring in each other and in the relationship. Remind your partner what your investment is ("I have been with you for___years, and I want this to work"), and that you care enough to resolve this problem so the two of you can go on happily together.

Step 3. Agree that a cooperative solution can be found.
Although you may have difficulty believing that a solution can be found that will satisfy both of you, declare out loud to each other that there must *be a way to cooperate in this situation, and you intend to do everything you can to find what it is. State that you care about your partner being satisfied, as well as you being happy with the eventual solution, and that you know that both of you need to be satisfied if the solution is to work.*

Establishing goodwill usually creates the atmosphere of mutual caring, trust, and teamwork that you need to feel cooperative, but if your problem is especially difficult, or if it is similar to a problem that caused major difficulty in a past relationship, or if you have a history of bitter struggles or fights instead of problem-solving, you or your partner may still feel anxious. As we discussed in Chapter 3 when one of you is anxious, that barrier can be overcome by reassurance.

Reassurance

Any disagreement between the two of you creates tension in what is probably the most significant and important relationship you have, so both you and your partner are likely to be somewhat anxious about the outcome of your negotiation. Reassuring each other reduces this anxiety, and, because you will both feel calmer, you will be able to think more clearly, be less likely to overreact emotionally, and therefore, cooperate more successfully.

You will use reassurance over and over in Cooperative Problem Solving, not only when you are Setting the Stage, but whenever your negotiating (or some other aspect of your relationship) becomes anxious, tense, or otherwise difficult. One can never be too expert at reassurance, it is like a fine oil that makes the gears of a relationship turn smoothly.

Whenever anxiety or fear show up in the form of defensiveness, competitiveness, resistance to negotiating, or tension between you, you can reduce it by following these guidelines:

Guidelines for Reassurance

1. Become aware of tension or difficulty. *If your conversation or negotiation begins to feel difficult, your partner is not being* *cooperative, or you find yourself feeling resistant and uncoopera-tive, it may be time for reassurance.*

2. Verify and discuss the emotional atmosphere. *Suggest to your partner that both your feelings seem to need some atten-tion, and describe how the emotional climate feels to you. If your partner seems to you to be anxious,* do not use "you" messages to tell your partner how he or she feels, *but use "I" messages describing what you feel, see, or experience that seems uncom-fortable, because "you" messages will increase the anxiety. If you think your partner is tense or anxious, ask for information.*

If Rose is aware that John has come home irritable, she can say, "Hi, Honey, How was your day?" This gives John an opening to express his tension or anxiety, and for Rose to find a way to reas-sure him. Or, if she is aware that she herself is tense, she can say, "John, I'm feeling anxious and stressed today. Will you help me understand it?"

In the middle of a negotiation, you might say, "I need to call a time-out. This discussion has begun to feel tense and strained. How are you feeling? Are you worried about something?" (alter-nately: "I am worried that..."). Once you have established and understood who is anxious or worried, and why, go on to the next step.

3. Identify and discuss reasons for tension. *The tension or anxiety between you or in the atmosphere will either be directly related to what you are discussing (and how you are interacting) or it will be brought in from another source (work stress, an argu-ment with someone else, bad commuting traffic). If your partner is anxious, use your Active Speaking and Active Listening skills (Chapter 3) as shown above, to find out what he or she thinks and feels.*

Ask your partner if he or she feels anxious, and if so, ask what it's about and use active listening and attentive speaking to find out if you are being misunderstood, as Rose does:

Rose: (opening discussion) *I'm really looking forward to talk-ing with you about the changes I want to make in my life.*

John: (arms folded across chest, unsmiling) *What are we supposed to do to work it out?*

Rose: (asking for information) *John, you look anxious. Are you worried about this?*

John: (admits he's anxious) *Yes, I don't see how these changes will do anything but create problems.*

Rose: (active listening) *Are you afraid you're life will change in ways you don't like?*

John: (confirming) *Yes.*

4. Offer or ask for reassurance. *Once the source of the tension and/or anxiety is identified, a specific reassurance is needed. For example, if you are anxious because you believe your partner is angry with you, you can ask to be reassured either that your partner is not angry, or that the anger can be resolved, and what you need to do to resolve it. Here, as in Steps 2 and 3, you will be using your communication skills to determine what reassurance to use. Sometimes the reassurance is spontaneous, as with Rose's response to John's fears:*

John: (realizing what he's tense about) *Maybe I'm afraid of losing you.*

Rose: (spontaneous, warm) *Oh, my dear, you couldn't lose me if you tried. I'll be with you for the rest of my life.*

John: (relieved, sighs) *Phew. That helps a lot. I thought you were getting more independent so you could eventually leave.*

Rose: (more considered reassurance) *I promise, John, if I ever want to leave, I'll tell you straight out, and not indirectly. Okay?*

John: (much more relaxed posture) *Okay. Now, I feel better about talking about this.*

5. Continue until the atmosphere becomes more relaxed. *Depending on how long-standing or intense the tension between you is, the above four steps can take a few minutes— or much longer. Continue discussing the anxiety, the reasons behind it, and the kind of reassurance that is needed until* *you feel the tension between you relax. You'll be able to tell this because the signs that indicated tension will change. For example, if you felt a knot in your stomach, your stomach will now feel relaxed. Or, if you felt the conversation was difficult and halting, it will now flow more smoothly. An atmosphere of heavy seriousness may lighten into laughter. When your original indicators of tension are relaxed, you are ready to resume the Cooperative Problem Solving process.* **Rose knew John was reassured when he let out a sigh of relief, and then his body relaxed.**

If you are unable to reassure each other, or repeated attempts at reassurance don't seem to help, suppressed hurt and anger from past conflicts may be coming to the surface. Try the following exercise for setting aside held anger and hurt, and come back to this step again later.

Barrier: Unresolved Anger and Hurt

If either you or your partner have had unsolved problems for a while, one or both of you may have a backlog of suppressed anger, frustration or hurt feelings: perhaps because you felt that expressing them would cause trouble or would accomplish nothing. These stored-up feelings can get in the way if they come out during negotiating because they create emotional and mental turmoil that can interfere with cooperation and with thinking clearly. Occasionally, held anger and hurt from some other incident (last week's fight about an unrelated issue) can also interfere if it gets in the way of your goodwill for one another and of your clear thinking.

Although your unresolved anger and hurt can emerge at any step in the negotiation, it will most often be revealed as you set the stage and one or both of you have trouble establishing goodwill, and reassurance doesn't seem to help.

Setting the Stage becomes impossible until held anger and hurt are resolved. Emotional turmoil creates an atmosphere that interferes with your thinking, and makes you see your partner as an enemy with whom you are more likely to lapse into arguing or power struggles and turn the negotiation into a competition.

It is inevitable that some hurt feelings and anger will arise in the course of a long-term relationship. Learning to set aside these intense feelings when you negotiate is not easy, but it is a very useful skill that will benefit you and your partner in many situations in addition to your negotiations, including at work, when problems arise with your children, or when emergencies must be handled in spite of intense feelings.

If Rose has been struggling with her discontent for some time and has had trouble getting John to take her seriously, she could have several months or even a year or two of hurt and resentment stored up about it:

> John: *Well, this is our negotiation date.* (establishing goodwill*) I love you, Rose, and I sure want to do what I can to make our life together the best it can be for both of us.*
>
> Rose: (bitterly) *Yeah, as long as it doesn't upset your tidy little nest.*
>
> John: (startled) *If you can't be civil, then I don't need this hassle.*
>
> Rose: (angry) *That's just your style. If it doesn't suit you, you refuse to deal!*
>
> **End of discussion.**

On the other hand, if Rose and John know about setting aside held anger and hurt, the evening can take quite another turn:

> **A little later.**
>
> Rose: (thoughtful) *John, I'm sorry I blew up a while ago. I took time to write and think about it, and I realized that I've been blaming you for my discontent and resenting that you wouldn't help me work out my problem. I'm not so angry now. In fact, I appreciate your trying to open the negotiation tonight, when it's my problem.*

John: (cautious) *I didn't realize you were so upset. Maybe we can try it again, but I think we both need a little more time to settle down and cool off. Can we take 15 minutes, and then come back to it?*

Rose: (agreeing) *I think that's a good idea. Let's have dessert and coffee, and then try again.*

Rose's held anger had been building for a while, and after it erupted, she took a break and wrote in her journal and thought about it. Once she had worked through her held anger, she was able to come back and explain herself to John, and ask to resume the negotiation. John had been caught by surprise, and his anger wasn't held very long, so after requesting a short additional break, he's ready to go again.

Setting Aside Held Anger and Hurt

If you or your partner are holding anger or hurt feelings regarding the problem you want to solve, or for any other reason, before you can proceed in your negotiation, a period of emotional discharge may be necessary. This discharge may be as simple as saying, "Wait a minute. I'm still angry about this, and I have to refocus on what we're doing." Or, if your anger and frustration has been long-standing, it may require taking a break in the negotiation at this point for the purpose of discharging or setting aside held anger and hurt. Also, it's important to remember that discharging *away from the person you're upset with* allows you to express your feelings in a way that doesn't aggravate the problem. Once you have resolved your feelings, you will be calm and able think clearly enough to return to your partner and solve the problem.

You and your partner can learn how to take time out to release and resolve anger, frustration, and hurt feelings in a variety of ways:

* Putting it aside temporarily by changing focus.
* Releasing your anger and hurt through physical activity.
* Releasing your anger and hurt by expressing your feelings through writing or talking.
* Releasing it by talking with a friend or therapist who will listen.

Depending on the intensity of your held hurt and anger, how long-standing it is, and how comfortable you are with handling your feelings, you can choose to discharge by yourself or with the help of another. Whichever you choose, remember, the partner who helped you generate the anger and hurt in the first place will probably not be able to listen objectively enough to help you discharge it.

Discharging by Yourself

Common levels of held anger or hurt (because they are not too overwhelming), can be discharged alone by writing down your feelings, talking out loud to yourself, and simply acknowledging how you feel as in the directions below. Many people think that feelings can only be discharged by "talking them out" with someone else (as in the directions below), and this is fine if you happen to have an *appropriate* friend handy when you need them, or are in therapy. But learning to discharge by yourself keeps you from being overly dependent on others, and is usually much simpler and less of an interruption in your problem-solving.

The advantages to releasing your held anger and hurt alone are:

1. You can do it when and where you want instead of waiting for the right friend or therapist to be available.
2. It is simpler than making arrangements with another person.
3. It may be easier to be more honest about your hurt and anger to yourself than to another.
4. You can choose a method that suits your personality and the nature of your problem.
5. It doesn't postpone your negotiation as much as making arrangements to talk to someone else does.

We recommend trying to discharge by yourself first, using the guidelines above, and if you find that your held anger and hurt are too intense for you to handle alone, *then* get the help of a friend or therapist.

Discharging With a Friend

Some people find it easier to release feelings by talking to someone because they feel heard, cared about, and validated, and they have someone's implicit permission to discharge. Also, because your friend is uninvolved in the problem, you know that your anger or hurt won't place pressure on or upset him or her. Very few good friends are objective enough to be good listeners, so when you choose someone, make sure they can hear you without judgment. The listener's role is to be nonjudgmental, dispassionate, and supportive. Also, you must be very careful *which* friend you choose to share your feelings with because you will be talking about your anger and hurt toward your partner. You need a friend who can understand that the feelings are temporary. Speak to someone who will listen to you without placing blame on either you or your partner, and who won't create problems by repeating what you said or bring it up later.

If attempting to discharge on your own doesn't help, call a friend, read the description of a good listener, and see if he or she will agree to help you. Then follow the instructions in the guidelines below.

Discharging With Professional Help

In cases where emotions have been pent up for a long time, involve repeated negative patterns (such as being abandoned, financially devastated, or cheated on) from past relationships, rape, violence, childhood neglect or abuse, or other traumatic history is involved, discharging held hurt and anger is critically important, needs knowledgeable supervision, and can take some time to complete. In these cases, getting into group or individual therapy is essential. If this describes you, and you are not in therapy, get a referral from a friend, a doctor, or a local hotline. Your therapist will help you through the guidelines below or similar methods of discharging.

Guidelines for Setting Aside Held Hurt and Anger

Step 1. Separate from the problem. *In order to discharge effectively, explain that you have held hurt and anger, request a time-out from problem-solving, and find a secure place to be alone, or with an uninvolved, neutral person. As we said above, this should be done away from your partner. To request a "time-out" in the negotiation, state that you're too angry, hurt, or tense to continue right now, and you want a break to take care of* *your feelings first. Set a new time and place to resume the discussion later, even another day if necessary, which will reassure your partner that the negotiation will continue, and that you are not using your hurt and anger to avoid negotiating permanently. Allow plenty of time to discharge your held feelings in one of the following ways. You can choose to do each of these options alone or with a friend or therapist, as previously explained.*

Step 2. Choose a method. *There are three methods of setting aside held anger and hurt, each of which is outlined in the exercises that follow. To choose the appropriate exercise for you, use the following simple exercises:*

A. Temporarily Setting Feelings Aside

B. Release Through Physical Activity

C. Release Through Verbal or Written Expression

Exercise A: Temporarily Setting Feelings Aside

This is the simplest of the options. John, for example, was able to take a few minutes, let his surprise and hurt subside, and simply focus on the negotiation again because his hurt wasn't long-standing or deep, but was a result of his conflict and misunderstanding with Rose earlier that same evening.

This is the best option to choose for a small upset, if you find it relatively easy to "postpone" dealing with your feelings and stay focused on problem-solving, with just a short (five to 15 minute) break. If your feelings are deeper and more intense, and you are not experienced at managing them, this may be too difficult to do.

This option is done by yourself and in your own mind:

1. Focus your mind, notice what you are feeling and acknowledge that it is an appropriate feeling.

2. See if you can set it aside for now (postpone expressing it), and continue the negotiation.

3. If you decide to postpone expressing it, focus on something that will motivate you to return to the discussion such as your desire to resolve the problem you are negotiating or your respect and love for your partner. Allow the anger or hurt to fade into the background as you move your attention to the task at hand.

4. Go on to Step 3 of the Guidelines.

Exercise B: Release Through Physical Activity

Choose this option if you enjoy physical activity and you often experience a change of mood after exercising. Emotions that are pent-up can often be released through physical activity, such as a brisk walk; dancing to music with a steady, pulsing beat; shooting baskets; bicycling, jogging; t'ai chi; yoga; swimming; wrestling; punching a pillow or a punching bag; or throwing something repeatedly in a safe setting. (A large, heavy phone book or catalog thrown at a soft bed or couch is energetic and safe, as is throwing or hitting a ball against a wall as in tennis, handball or racquetball, or beating a mattress with a tennis racket or a bat.)

When you begin your "workout," you may feel your held emotion as tension in your body, usually the midsection area: stomach, chest, shoulders, back, neck, head, or jaws. The exercise will loosen the muscles holding the tension and allow you to release some of the held emotion, so you can get back to negotiating.

1. Choose an exercise from the above examples, or your favorite physical activity, and set aside a time to handle these feelings through that activity.

2. As you exercise, pay attention to your feelings and whatever tension you feel in your body, and try to continue your workout until the intensity of your hurt and anger are reduced and you can reconnect with the good feelings you have toward your partner, and can focus on the task of problem-solving.

3. Go to Step 3 of the Guidelines.

Exercise C: Release Through Verbal or Written Expression

Choose this option if you often use writing or talking out loud (to yourself or to a friend) to help you understand how you feel and what you want to do. Held emotions are exactly that—held. When you express them they lose their pent-up energy, and become much more easy to deal with and set aside.

1. Find a place to be alone and uninterrupted for whatever time you need to write or talk your feelings out. Your held anger and hurt can be expressed in whatever way feels best to you: write, yell, talk, or cry. If you are alone, you can write or draw in your journal, talk or yell (into a tape recorder, if you wish) out loud. The more you allow yourself to express what you are angry or hurt about, the easier it will be to let those feelings go, and get on to the business of solving the problem.

2. Once you have written or talked enough to understand your feelings and decide what to do about them, go to Step 3 of the Guidelines.

Step 3. Wait for a release. *Keep expressing your feelings in your chosen way until you feel a "letting go" or release. This is the discharge, and you'll know when you get to it because you'll experience a feeling of relief. Along with the relief, you may also discover the "real" or central reason for the feelings, which often spontaneously comes in the form of a new idea. It is often accompanied by an "Aha!" feeling of discovery, or a "Whew!" feeling of relief.* For example, John told himself how angry he was while he took a shower, and after a few minutes, he suddenly realized "Oh! I'm angry at Rose because she surprised me by being angry when I was ready to negotiate, and feeling my caring for her. I felt ambushed. When she apologized, I wasn't ready to forgive her yet. I think I'm ready now, because it doesn't seem so important anymore."

When you feel your tension release, you'll find that your thinking capacity returns, and you can go on with problem-solving, either by yourself or with the other person. You will now be able to think clearly enough to use your autonomous thinking and effective choice-making to solve the problem, so you are ready to resume negotiating as you agreed.

Mastering these skills, and the steps of Setting the Stage (*set time and place, establish goodwill, reassure, and set aside held anger and hurt*), will enable you to create a calm, mutually caring, cooperative, and inviting atmosphere in which it will be easy to think clearly and solve the problem.

Being able to create this atmosphere whenever you want to is a valuable skill that will greatly enhance your Cooperative Problem Solving efforts.

Once you have completed the steps to Setting the Stage, you are ready to move on to the final phases of Cooperative Negotiation. In the next chapter, you will learn to State Your Wants, a key step of the Negotiating Tree, where you and your partner communicate exactly what you want. This is the step where you will become clear about where you are in agreement and where you are in conflict.

## Chapter 5

State Your
Wants

Once you have set the stage, you and your partner can focus on solving the problem, as a team, without being distracted by old anger and hurt, or by interruptions. Stating and Exploring Wants is the first step of the Negotiation Tree where you *both* begin to contribute to the problem-solving process, by participating equally in stating what you want.

Stating Wants in a helpful, nonthreatening way is critical to solving the problem because it helps both you and your partner understand the differences and similarities in the way you want this problem solved, and what it will take to satisfy each of you. If you don't know what your partner wants, you can wind up with a "false" or one-sided solution, that will leave one or both of you feeling unsatisfied, overpowered, or manipulated. Stating Wants is like putting all the true facts on the table, just as you lay all the pieces of a jigsaw puzzle out, so you can see them better, and more easily to solve your puzzle.

Much of the confusion about expressing wants occurs because no distinction is made between *wanting* and *demanding*. Stating what you want is an effort to communicate clearly, so you and your partner can both be satisfied, while demanding is insisting that your partner *give* you what you want, without regard for his or her wants and feelings.

Demanding is driven by a belief in scarcity and fear of not getting enough. The important difference between knowing what you want and demanding that others give it to you, or manipulating others to get it, is that knowing what you want is cooperative, and contributes to successful problem-solving. Demanding and manipulating are competitive and create a struggle.

This confusion between wanting and demanding can cause you to suppress your awareness of your wants and desires, which makes it difficult, if not impossible, to satisfy them.

Your natural wanting has probably been suppressed if:

* You go "blank" when you try to think of what you want.
* You believe you "don't care" what the result is, but you feel unhappy or resentful later.
* You feel dissatisfied, but you can't put your feeling into words, or think what to do about it.
* You get anxious, depressed or angry when a problem needs to be solved, because you feel you'll "lose."
* You want what everyone else wants, what you think you "should" want, or what someone else has, but you can't think of what you want on your own.

The Importance of Wanting

As adults we are responsible for satisfying our own needs and seeing to our own wants, and if we don't know what we want, we'll have trouble getting it and experience a lifelong feeling of deprivation, disappointment, scarcity, and resentment. Feeling you can't have what you want makes it difficult to express true generosity or support for your partner to have what he or she wants. Your enthusiasm, creativity, and motivation to try and solve problems would be stifled if you believed there was no way to get what you want. Not knowing what you want, therefore, creates a false sense of scarcity, and also creates competition. When there appears to be a shortage (as in a gasoline shortage), competitive people don't try to solve the problem so everyone can be satisfied (share cars, use alternative transportation), but compete for the limited supply. Knowing (and saying) what you want is essential to solving problems successfully within your relationship, because only then can you work together to come up with a mutually satisfactory solution.

Even more importantly, when partners state their wants, they often discover, to their amazement, that their wants are quite similar, and the problem disappears. The conflict between them was only their lack of understanding and communication. Until they were honest about what they wanted, each assumed the other wanted something different. In simple negotiations, after both partners have stated what they want, they may find that they're essentially in agreement, and the problem will then easily be solved.

In the last chapter, John and Rose had Set the Stage for their negotiation, and now it's after supper, and they're settling down to talk, but neither of them has taken the time to think about what they want:

> **John:** (taking responsibility and cooperating in the negotiation) *Okay, Rose, you said you had a problem now that the kids were grown, and you felt unneeded. What do you think would fix it?*
>
> **Rose:** (vague) *Oh, I don't know. Maybe we could do more together.*
>
> **John:** (defensive) *Rose, you know that's not possible. I'm too busy at work. Be realistic.*
>
> **Rose:** (feeling helpless and confused) *I'm just so depressed. I don't know what to do.*
>
> **John:** (taking over) *You need to go see a doctor, like I said before.*
>
> **Rose:** (giving up) *Oh, I guess you're right.*
>
> **End of discussion.**

As a result of not Stating and Exploring Wants, both Rose and John are confused and vague, unable to discuss what they want specifically enough to reach a solution, so they end up discouraged and frustrated, and less inclined to believe that negotiation will work. On the other hand, if Rose and John are following the Negotiation Tree and they take the time to get clear on what they want, the discussion goes differently:

John: (taking responsibility and cooperating in the negotiation) *Okay, Rose, you said you had a problem now that the kids were grown, and you felt unneeded. What do you think would fix it?*

Rose: (clearly stating what she wants) *Well, John, I've been thinking about it, and I know I want to find something meaningful to do. I'm a caretaker by nature, and I'm sure someone can use my skills. At the same time, I don't want to disrupt our relationship, or make you unhappy. I know you're used to having me here. So, I need to find out what's most important to you about the way we've always done things.*

John: (stating his wants) *Rose, I am aware that you're unhappy, and I would much prefer to see you happy. But, you've always been my support system, and I don't want to lose that. I want to be able to call you up and ask you to do something for me, or bring home business associates for dinner, or just have my usual dinner at the usual time. It really lessens my job stress to have your support.*

Rose: (considering possibilities) *That doesn't sound too difficult. If I volunteered or took some classes, I might not always be able to be there at the very moment you want me, but I was often gone when the kids had to go to the doctor or something, and we always worked that out. Maybe we could work this out, too.*

Rose and John find when they remain calm and centered, and clearly state their wants, they are not so far apart. The energy they would have previously lost to arguing can be put into carrying out the solution to the problem.

On the other hand, if you are used to competing rather than cooperating when faced with a problem, what you and your partner want can *appear* to be so different and seem so incompatible that solving the problem will look impossible at first. But, if you persevere and complete the whole Cooperative Problem Solving process, you will realize that discovering how different your wants are does not mean they're unsolvable.

Summarizing Rose's and John's wants, the "facts" might look like this:

Rose	John
I want something meaningful to do.	I want you to be a support system for me: run errands, prepare meals, and entertain business associates.
I want more time for me.	I want you to be available, as you always have been.
I want to preserve our marriage	I want to preserve our marriage.
I want you to be happy, too.	I want you to be happy, too.

Now that their wants are clearly expressed, Rose and John can understand each other. The problem is clear, which will make it easier to proceed to developing their options for solving it. The normal tendency for many people would be to worry about how far apart some of their wants seem. However, in Cooperative Problem Solving, we do not focus on the difference in this step, because that would tempt us to censor our wants and make it difficult to figure out and communicate what we want. The emphasis here is on what wants would have to be satisfied for you to be happy.

Skills for Stating Your Wants

In Stating and Exploring Wants, you will develop the following skills:

* You'll become aware of everything you want.
* You'll learn to communicate it clearly to your partner.
* You'll learn to listen to your partner's wants without making assumptions, getting discouraged, jumping to conclusions, or getting anxious.

In this chapter you will learn what to do if you become stuck in your negotiation, and how to keep yourselves motivated and hopeful about the solution. The exercises will help you explore your wants and your attitudes about wanting, in order to clear the way to having what you want, while ensuring that your partner has his or her wants satisfied.

Barriers to Stating Wants

When you State Your Wants, you may be surprised to find yourself beginning to compete with each other rather than cooperate. This competitiveness can be triggered by your anxiety about the differences in your wants. Cooperation is important in this step of the Negotiation Tree because a competitive attitude can derail your negotiation and cause you to fall back into the old habit of rescuing your mate by not stating your wants fully and clearly. Or you may create a power struggle over who will get their way if you don't listen to your partner's wants.

If you object to the wants your partner expresses, or try to explain why they won't work, or criticize them, you won't fully understand what your partner's wants are. Even if you say nothing, but carry on a silent, mental commentary on what your partner wants, you will not understand or hear them properly. Your partner has a reason to want whatever he or she wants, and you must know that reason in order to effectively negotiate. Arguing with your partner's wants either verbally or silently makes it impossible to hear and understand your partner's position.

If you allow yourself to become afraid that your wants are too different and slide back into old power struggles or rescuing while Stating and Exploring Your Wants, you may:

* *Exaggerate your want* (power struggle): The fear that you may not get what you want may cause you to say you want more than you really do ("I want you here all the time"). You'll be reacting to the scarcity-based belief that, at best, you'll only get part of what you ask for. This is confusing to both you and your partner, and because your wants are exaggerated, makes it look much more difficult to reach a satisfactory solution than it really is.
* *Overstate your need* (power struggle): The fear that you won't get your wants met if they are "just wants" may cause you to state what you want as if your survival depended on

it ("I'll just DIE if you don't come with me"). This causes your partner to feel suspicious that he or she is being manipulated, and resist cooperating with you.

* *Argue for or justify your want* (power struggle): Anxiety that your wants are not important enough to be satisfied may lead you to present them as a persuasive argument, with an overwhelming flood of reasons *why* you *should* want them or that the wants should be satisfied ("I should get more of the money than you do, because..."). This can provoke your partner to object and argue in return, rather than listen.

* *Not say what you want* (rescue): Belief that you won't get what you want anyway, or that differences in wants will cause a fight, may lead you to say you "don't care" or "it's not important" or just be silent, when the truth is you'll resent not getting what you want.

* *Understate your want* (rescue): Fear that your partner will be upset, hurt, or unhappy if you say what you really want may lead you to ask for something else ("I want to go to a movie," when you really want an evening all alone together) or something less. This confuses your partner, and makes it impossible to solve the problem for what you really want (because you haven't said what it is).

By not clearly stating what you want, you make it impossible for your partner to clearly understand your position, and, as Don and Dale discover, create competition and struggle rather than cooperation and a mutually satisfying solution.

Don and Dale have defined the problem: both of them want the back bedroom for an office, and they set the stage for their negotiation, but when they try to solve the problem, they run into trouble:

Don: (stating want) *I want to use the back bedroom for my office. I'm spending too much on office space.*

Dale: (stating want, beginning to justify) *I want to use the back bedroom for my office, too, because from there I can keep an eye on Kendra as she plays in the backyard.*

Don: (gets competitive) *I could always keep an eye on her, and you could use the dining room. Besides, you only work part time, and I work full time, so I deserve it more.*

Dale: (getting angry, arguing) *The dining room is dark and everyone tramps through it all the time coming in and out and I think it's about time I had a decent place to work. Besides, if you ran your business better, you'd easily be able to afford the rent on the office you already have.*

Don and Dale find themselves in an argument, and no longer negotiating about what they want, because they *aren't listening* to each other; and they're both locked in competing, trying to "win." They have reverted to believing in scarcity and both assume that only one of them will get what he wants.

When Don and Dale remember to use "I" messages and active listening, focus on stating their own wants, listen more carefully to each other, and support each other in stating their wants, the discussion has a better outcome:

Don: (stating want) *I want to use the back bedroom for my office. My business isn't doing as well as it was, and I need to cut my expenses.*

Dale: (active listening) *Well, I understand that you want that room for an office. It would be cheaper for you. (stating want) I want it too. I want to be where it's quiet and has more light, and also where I can watch Kendra play in the yard.*

Don: (active listening) *You want more light, less traffic and noise, and to be able to see Kendra in the yard?*

Dale: (confirms) *Right. It sounds like our wants are clear. Is there anything you'd like to add?*

Don: *Only that it also sounds great to work here, from home.*

Dale: *It sounds good to me, too.*

Don: (ready for the next step) *Okay, shall we explore our options? Let's put our heads together and see if there's a way we can both get what we want.*

Dale: *Yes. I think we can do it.*

Don and Dale's first attempt became competitive, because they became afraid that one of them would "lose," and they began arguing with each other about *why* one of them deserved the office more. In the second attempt, they began to cooperate, acting on the assumption that they could find a mutually satisfactory solution, and seeking to work together.

Using active listening and "I" messages, they were able to stay focused on stating their wants and hearing each other, without jumping to conclusions or arguing, and therefore keep their focus on solving the problem to their *mutual* satisfaction.

To get both your wants satisfied, each of you must first state clearly what you want: to communicate what you want, you must first *know* what you want.

The Importance of Knowing What You Want

You may be wondering why being clear about what you and your partner want is getting so much emphasis here. Many people have serious trouble knowing what they want, feeling comfortable communicating it, and stating it clearly to a partner. We have found that many couples have difficulty solving problems because they do not know what they want, or, if they do know, cannot express it to a partner. If that's a problem for either or both of you, then these skills are what you need to learn to build a lasting, sustainable relationship.

In their desire to help us become more social and generous adults (which all small children need to learn), who were also raised to be competitive and believe in scarcity, often give us the idea (by being stressed, anxious, guilty, or angry if they are not able to give us what we want) that our wants are wrong. As a result, we often grow up suppressing our desires: sometimes to the extent of not even being aware of them. As grown-ups, we carry these early childhood rules, admonitions, and restrictions with us in the often unconscious form of habits, beliefs, and maxims that we live by.

A child who wants to be loved and approved of, and who realizes that wanting things makes Mommy or Daddy unhappy, worried, upset, or angry, will eventually learn to shut the wanting off. First, you learn not to say what you want, because it upsets someone. After a few months or years, not being able to express your desires becomes too painful to endure, and you learn to shut them out of your awareness.

Most of us are taught, from early childhood on, that our wants are selfish and that we should be polite and let others wants come first ("Be polite, let Susie have the toy"). We are made to feel that it isn't okay to want ("Don't even *ask* me for a cookie just before dinner"), or that we can't have what we want ("*Of course* you can't have a new toy, do you think I'm made of money?") or that, if we get what we want, someone else will be deprived (a belief in scarcity). In response, some of us learn (perhaps in competition with brothers and sisters) to grab what we can get, without considering whether we want it or not.

Even when we grow up and have the power to get most of what we want for ourselves, we continue to act these beliefs as though we were not in charge of getting what we want. These internalized "shoulds," "should nots," and restrictions make us anxious about getting what we want and even convinced that we won't. This in turn leads us to compete, to rescue, and to otherwise prevent ourselves from clearly knowing and stating what we want. Cooperative Problem Solving can help us to come up with creative and effective ways to get it.

In addition to all these other restrictions on wanting, you may have the idea that the consequences of wanting are bad (no one will like you), and so it is too scary to know what you want. Because knowing what you want sometimes means you risk being disappointed (there may be a real reason why you can't get it), and many people have an exaggerated idea of how bad disappointment feels (if I don't get what I want I'll be miserable), they avoid wanting at all (thus unconsciously guaranteeing that they won't be able to get it, because you can't negotiate for a want you don't know about).

If you have any of these difficulties being aware of what you want, and communicating it to your partner, the following exercises will help you restore your natural, healthy wanting, and communicate your wants to your partner.

This series of seven steps is designed to break down the barriers that impede your awareness of what you want, to help you activate your natural ability to want, and recover wants you may have suppressed since childhood. As you follow the steps, you will discover the ways you stifle your wants and develop alternatives so that you can easily know and communicate what you want in Cooperative Problem Solving. If you have a lot of trouble with wanting, you may wish to repeat it several times, over a period of days or weeks, until you become completely comfortable with identifying and accepting your wants.

Exercise: Steps to Clarifying Your Wants

If you are doing these exercises with your partner you can take turns reading the instructions. You will need to set aside 15 to 30 minutes at a time and place where you won't be interrupted. You will need a pencil and paper.

These first two steps use the "magic" of a wizard or fairy god-mother to bypass the internalized "shoulds" and restrictions that limit and control your ability to know what you want.

Step 1. Discovering your childhood wants. *Read this exercise slowly, pausing where you see three dots in a row to allow time for the fantasy to form. You may find it easier to tape record the instructions and play them back to give freedom to your imagination.*

Do not stifle your wants by criticizing or questioning them or insisting that they be logical or make sense, but allow them to come out as they are: impossible or fantastic wishes are okay. If grown-up wants show up, let them, but do the best you can to stay in touch with being a child while you make your wishes.

Close your eyes and picture yourself as a young child, about 7 years old...alone in a favorite place from your childhood.... You might see your child self in your room...or outdoors in a special hiding place...where you used to go.... Now pretend a wizard (or a magician, a genie, or a fairy godmother) comes to you...and says you can have any wishes you can name in five minutes.... Allow your 7-year-old self to imagine anything at all.... What do you imagine? What do you wish for...? Wish for all the material things you want...toys, ice cream, new in-line skates, jewels, money...wish for love and happiness, praise and encouragement...wish for friends your own age, and grown-up people who care about you...whatever you want.

Now, slowly open your eyes, review what just happened in your fantasy, and write down your wants. Head the page "My Child-hood Want List."

Here's how Joe's Childhood Want List looked:

My Childhood Want List:

* A sailboat.

* Cowboy boots.

* Plenty of time to play.

* Never have to go to the dentist.

* Lots of money.

* Fly a plane.

* To be a baseball pro.

* To be Superman.

* Have a Batmobile.

* Lots of hugs and snuggles.

* A secret friend to have a clubhouse with.

This list has some possible and impossible ideas on it, all quite natural for the 7-year-old Joe, which shows that he's in touch with his natural, childlike ability to want, and able to be cre-ative without judging and stifling what he wants. If your list sounds childlike, you are getting in touch with your natural abil-ity to want; if your wants sound too adult ("I want more stabil-ity in my life," "a better job"), repeat the exercise and spend more time on establishing your picture of a 7-year-old you.

Having experienced your child self's wants and how it feels to be in "wanting mode," you are ready for Step 2, which will focus on your present-day grown-up wants and help you up-date your want list.

Step 2. Discovering your wants today. *Again, do not criticize or question your wants: allow them to come out as they are. Allow your self to imagine anything at all, no matter how impossible,* *illogical, or fantastic it sounds. If an item comes up expressed in terms of "I don't want...." that's okay, too.*

Now, fantasize as you did before, but this time see yourself as the grown-up you are today: Close your eyes, and picture yourself as you are now...alone in that same favorite place from your childhood...a special hiding place...where you used to go.... Now pretend a wizard (or a magician, a genie, or a fairy godmother) comes to you...and says you can have any wishes you can name in five minutes...what do you wish for...? Wish for all the material things you want...a sports car, a boat, a mink, to win the lottery, be very famous...and also the nonmaterial: love and happiness, success, praise and encouragement...wish for friends, people who care about you, good sex.... Now, slowly open your eyes, review what just happened in your fantasy Head your list "My Wants Today" and write down your wishes.

Here's what Joe's grown-up list might look like:

My Wants Today:

* $6,000/ month net pay.
* A sailboat.
* Not to work.
* Not to feel stressed.
* Not to worry about money.
* No relationship hassles.
* Cowboy boots.
* A thriving business consulting and teaching.
* Six months off every year.
* '55 Chevy—cherry condition
* Uninhibited sex with Michelle.
* New computer with graphics.
* To play professional baseball.
* Travel—Jamaica, African safari.
* Live in a small town.
* Season tickets to football.

* Mountain bike.

* To fly my own Lear jet.

Similar to Joe's grown-up list, yours will probably be different from your child list, but contain some related things. Some of the items on your list, as on Joe's, may not seem possible (a Lear jet, for example), but it belongs on the list anyway, because it is a want.

The next three steps will deepen your understanding of your internal restrictions, and help you know, express, and communicate your true wants by exposing and counteracting the "shoulds" that prevent you from knowing what you want.

Step 3. Overcoming the Barriers to Wanting. *Review and contemplate both your childhood and your adult want list. As you do this, reasons why you can't have some of your wants will probably come up, or thoughts that the wishes are silly, childish, greedy, not nice, selfish, or wrong. You may think "we can't afford it," or "you don't deserve that, you haven't been good." These internal reasons for not wanting are what you need to discover and counteract to free up your ability to know what you want. Write down all the reasons you think you can't have what you want in a column opposite your wants, and try not to censor or argue with these negative thoughts, to bring them into your awareness and find out what they are.*

When Joe looked at his lists, his internal restrictions and objections sounded like this:

(COLUMN 1) What Do I Want?	(COLUMN 2) What's in the Way?
$6,000/ month net pay.	Not worth the effort. Can't earn that much.
A sailboat.	Can't afford it.
Cowboy boots.	Won't use them enough.
A thriving business consulting and teaching.	Can't do a business by myself.

Six months off.

' 55Chevy—cherry condition.

Uninhibited sex with Michelle.

New computer with graphics.

Travel—Jamaica, African safari.

Play professional baseball.

Live in a small town.

Season tickets to football.

Mountain bike.

To fly my own Lear jet.

Can't afford it.

Silly—kids stuff.

She'll never change.

Sex dies out in long-term relationships.

Too much money.

Too much money, no time.

Too old, not enough skill.

Can't earn a living.

Too expensive.

I'll probably get hurt.

Don't deserve it.

Can't afford it.

After your list is created, evaluate how realistic your restrictions and objections are. When Joe wrote his restrictions they seemed true because he has believed them for a long time, but as he reviewed them objectively and thought about them, he realized he felt differently about them; some were obviously false ("I don't deserve it"), some were probably not true ("I'll probably get hurt"), some were actually true ("too old, not enough skill to play pro ball"), and some were temporarily true ("I can't afford it"). Go through your own list again, and mark whether the objections are (F) false, (PF) probably false, (TT) temporarily true, or (T) true. Now, in order to begin to eliminate some of your inner restrictions and open yourself to your true wants:

* When an objection is false (F), cross it out, and let your want stand uncorrected.

* When an objection is probably false (PF), make a note about what you need to do to make sure it's not true (Joe wrote: "Get information about mountain bike safety, join a mountain bike club").

* When one is temporarily true (TT), make some notes about what you'd have to do to make it false, (Joe wrote: get more education, get a better job, win the lottery).

When you find one that is true, see if you can alter the want or circumstance a bit until your objections become false (Joe can't be a professional ballplayer, but he can join an amateur league).

Joe's "in the way" list reveals some wants that actually are impossible. "Playing professional baseball" is not possible, at Joe's age, [Joe's objection gets a (T)] and Joe never had professional-level skill. But, adjusting the want a little bit and joining a baseball or softball league in his age group is still very possible, and might provide him with lots of satisfaction.

Other things that he has on the list, such as owning a sailboat, may not be possible immediately, (TT) but, if he wants to put in the effort, he could buy a used one and fix it up, or get some friends to share the cost of a sailboat. After research, Joe finds that season tickets to football are NOT too expensive, and crosses that objection out.

In this way, Joe is able to remove some of his reasons for not wanting and open up some possibilities on his want list.

Step 4. What's scary about wanting? *You may find that when you begin to explore what you want, you feel vaguely afraid, as if it's wrong to want things too strongly or clearly.*

You may have old beliefs left over from childhood that say it's greedy, bad, hopeless, or wrong to want things, or that bad things will happen to you, or you'll be terribly disappointed if you want them too strongly. These are not objections to individual things that you want, but objections to wanting itself.

Write down your own ideas and fantasies about what you think are the bad things that might happen if you want too much. Keep writing things down until you feel you have captured the scariest possible ideas on your paper. Joe's list follows as an example.

What Am I Afraid Will Happen If I Want Too Much?

* If I get all the things I want there will probably be a catch.
* I'll want things I can't have and be disappointed and dissatisfied.

* To have all that stuff, I'd have to be rich, and to get rich, I'd have to do things that are not nice ("con" people, exploit customers or employees, cheat on taxes, rob a bank).

* People who get everything they want mostly steal from others, and don't care about others. They are not liked, and they die rich and lonely.

* God will punish me if I get too greedy.

* Something bad will happen.

You can see that, with fears like these, Joe might have a difficult time allowing himself to know what he wants. However, once these fears, which are left over from childhood, are brought into awareness, they can be resolved, counteracted, and reassured, so that you are free to know what you want, and therefore, know how to solve your problem.

Step 5. Counteracting your fear. *Look at your list of reasons you can't have what you want. Imagine that you are encouraging and supporting a very dear friend of yours. If your friend gave you reasons (such as Joe's or yours) why he or she couldn't have what he wanted and be happy, would you accept them without question and advise him or her to give up hope? Chances are you would tell your friend that it is perfectly possible to have everything on the list and be happy, honest, and well-loved, too. You would explain why you thought his reasons for not getting what he wants were wrong, and reassure his fears by suggesting solutions for them which are encouraging, and stimulate his hope, creativity and clearer thinking.*

By doing two things, you can learn to reassure yourself when your objections to wanting get in the way.

1. For each fear on your list, find a solution. That is, consider what you might do to:

A. Solve the fearful outcome if it happens.

B. Avoid it happening in the first place.

C. Be more creative about finding a non-fearful way of getting what you want.

D. Reassure or rebut your dire prediction.
2. Write these solutions next to your fears.
Here's how Joe counteracted his scary list:

What Is Scary About Wanting?

How to Take the Fear Out

I'll want all the things I can't have and be disappointed and dissatisfied. I'll be miserable.

I can look more closely at my wants to see which ones I want enough to actually get. I can divide them into easy, medium, and difficult categories, and I can meet as many of my wants as I can, enjoy those, and not let the others spoil my fun.

To have all that stuff, I'd have to be rich, and to get rich, I'd have to do things that are not nice ("con" people, exploit customers or employees, cheat on taxes, rob a bank).

I can be rich, honest, and fair, too. There are honest ways to make money. I could use my wealth to benefit the community. Or, I can decide I don't want to do what it would take to get things, that it isn't worth the hassle, and be happy about it.

People who get everything they want mostly steal from others, and don't care about others. They are not liked, and they die rich and lonely.

Not true. Many of the best things in life can't be bought with money. People also get legitimately successful in business, inherit, win lotteries, and are loved.

Once you have counteracted each fear, you are ready to replace it with encouragement. Step 6 will help you overcome fears that may keep your wants suppressed.

Step 6. What's good about what I want. *Use each item in your "solutions" list in a statement that uses it as the solution to your fears about wanting. Joe's solutions looked like this:*
* In order to get what I want, I must first know what I want.
* If I had lots of money, I could help my friends and others who are needy.

* Wanting not to take advantage of people makes me proud.

* Whether I'm rich or not, I don't want to hurt anyone.

* I can have love in my life whether or not I have money.

* I know people who know what they want, go for it, and are happy.

* Even if what I want seems impossible now, I can probably do it step by step.

You can use these positive statements to encourage yourself and to show your partner how to encourage you (this works for both partners) whenever you need support in wanting.

Sometimes, all you can think of is what you don't want. In that case, go on to Step 7, which will help you figure out how to turn a "don't want" into a "want."

Step 7. Getting from "don't want" to "want." *If you're still having trouble figuring out what you want, knowing what you don't want can help, because you can turn it around into what you do want. Review your Wants Today list, in Step 2, and pick out anything you listed as something you don't want, or, if you are presently negotiating, and can only think of what you don't want, use that.*

Joe's "don't wants" are:

* Not to work,

* Not to feel stressed,

* Not to worry about money,

* No relationship hassles.

Now, take your "don't want" list, and opposite each item, list the want that's implied in the "don't want." For example, "I don't want to hurt any more" becomes " I want to feel happy and secure."

Following is Joe's turned around list.

Not to work.	*BECOMES*	*Have plenty of money.*
Not to feel stressed.	*BECOMES*	*Learn to be relaxed.*
Not to worry about money.	*BECOMES*	*Have more money, learn how to manage it better, or just lighten up about it.*
No relationship hassles.	*BECOMES*	*Learn to solve problems with Michelle better, have more fun.*

Once you know how to turn a "don't want" into a want you can do this anytime you or your partner can only come up with what you don't want.

Even when you know what you want, it isn't always easy to communicate your wants clearly to your partner. You may have difficulty expressing your want, because you are worried about your partner's reaction to it. Or it may be difficult for you to hear and understand your partner's wants because you're too concerned about what you want. To solve the problem cooperatively, however, each of you needs to know what the other one wants.

Communicating Wants

Most people who know clearly what they want, but have problems expressing it to their partner, are usually using old competitive habits such as:

1. Overstating or exaggerating wants (power struggle).
2. Understating wants to avoid conflict or please a partner (rescue).
3. Using "you" messages such as "you have to stop putting me down" instead of "I" messages such as "I want to feel more respected by you" (communication skills).
4. Speaking from accumulated hurt and anger that sounds like blaming or complaining; such as an angry, "I want to feel

appreciated around here once in a while!" instead of a calm "I do a lot for our partnership and I want to know you appreciate it."

5. Being afraid to say what you want, because of "shoulds" that make you feel it's wrong.

These restrictions on *saying* what you want, like the restrictions on *knowing* what you want, are confusing. The resulting confusion distorts your ideas of what will solve the problem and prevents you from solving the problem to get what both of you *really* want.

You have already learned about most of the communication skills that overcome these problems ("I" messages, Active Listening, Attentive Speaking, and Reassurance) in Chapter 3. The following guidelines will help you use your new communication skills when you have a problem to solve and you need to State Your Wants.

If you and your partner are having trouble communicating your wants, the following five steps will help you effectively take the extra time you need to make sure your wants are clear to each other, so you can understand exactly what will solve the problem and then, by continuing to follow the Negotiation Tree, you can find a mutually satisfactory solution.

Guidelines for Sharing Wants

Guideline 1: Set the stage *(Chapter 4). If the atmosphere of mutual cooperation you originally created by Setting the Stage has deteriorated, and you are feeling frustrated, competitive or discouraged, recreate a positive atmosphere by repeating that step. Make sure you have plenty of time and a private place, establish your good feelings about your relationship and each other, and set aside hurt and anger for the purpose of the discussion. This will make it much easier to think clearly, communicate well, and hear each other, because you will begin by being calm and reassured.*

Guideline 2: Use your communication skills *(Chapter 3). One partner speaks first, expressing their wants in the form of "I" messages. Using Attentive Speaking to be sure your wants* *are being heard will make expressing your wants much more effective and efficient. The other partner will try to "hear" all these wants, using Active Listening to reassure the first partner that they hear what he or she is saying. Then switch, so the first partner to speak now becomes the listener.*

Guideline 3: Reassure each other *(Reassurance Guidelines, Chapter 3). When you or your partner show signs of needing reassurance (gets silent, withdraws, argues), do these three things:*

1. Use active listening and attentive speaking to find out your partner's fears.

2. Reassure your partner with the positive messages from Step 6 of the Clarifying Your Wants Exercise (page 181).

3. Give direct answers about what you'll do if the worst happens, as in the Guidelines to calm the situation down and get back to sharing your wants.

Guideline 4: Remember that you are sharing wants—not trying to resolve conflict. *At this stage, your only task is to understand what your partner wants, and communicate what you want. Questioning your partner's wants, arguing with or criticizing what your partner wants, or suggesting solutions, is premature and will create defensiveness and competitiveness between you. Working out any differences you have comes in a later step in the Negotiation Tree.*

Guideline 5: Say exactly what you want, not more, not less. *Monitor what you say to be sure you are not using any of the barriers to Wanting (exaggerating, understating, overstating, justifying or arguing, or not saying your wants) to avoid or manipulate your partner's response. If you find that you're creating a barrier, or you get confused about what you want, go back to the Clarifying Wants exercise and review them, then come back to your partner and restate them as clearly and calmly as you can.*

As you become more adept at Stating Your Wants, you'll find that because you care about *each other's* wants, it is easier to maintain an attitude of cooperation, and avoid struggling or competing.

Knowing what you want, being able to communicate that clearly with your partner, and turning your "don't wants" into "wants" helps each of you to be better understood, and makes it easier for both of you to work together to get *both* your wants met. This frees you to move on to the final steps of the Negotiation Tree: Exploring Options and Deciding, which will show you how to fulfill both your own and your partner's wants.

## Chapter 6

Explore Your Options and Decide

In State Your Wants, you and your partner learned to identify and communicate what you want. Once you understand each others wants clearly, you will discover one of three things:

1. *The solution is obvious.* Your wants are so similar or compatible that the solution is obvious, and the problem is solved. It was merely your lack of understanding, miscommunication, or lack of awareness that created the problem. When that happens, it's not necessary to explore options because the problem is already solved for you, as in the case of John and Rose's problem in Chapter 5. If clarifying your wants has led you to believe that your problem is virtually solved, you can skip directly to the section called Decide and Confirm Your Decision (page 215).

2. *Your wants seem compatible.* Your wants seem similar enough to be easily reconciled, but you haven't come to a definite solution. In this case, you will feel reassured by knowing what you both want, and proceed to creatively explore new options (brainstorm) and discuss them until the solution becomes clear. *When Carol and Joe clarified their wants about housework, they realized they both wanted someone else to do it,*

which was compatible, but they still have to come up with a solution.

3. *Your wants seem in conflict or unsolvable.* Often, although your wants are clear and mutually understood, they are conflicting and a mutually satisfactory solution isn't obvious. *Paul might want a beach vacation (to swim and relax in the sun) while Mary wants to go to the mountains (to hike and get exercise and clean air). Fred might want sex three times a week, and Naomi might prefer once every two weeks. Don and Dale might struggle over what seems like not enough space in the house for both of them to have their offices there.*

When your wants conflict, finding a mutually satisfactory solution is more difficult than when they are compatible, but not at all impossible. In this chapter, you will learn to find a workable, mutually satisfying solution and avoid your old, competitive habits, such as power plays and rescues. Explore Your Options and Decide is the part of the Negotiation Tree that most of us think of as the "problem-solving" part of solving a problem—developing possible solutions, determining the best options, and making a decision.

Explore Your Options and Decide is usually the easiest step of the Negotiation Tree, and the most fun because you have done all the work of creating an atmosphere of cooperation, mutual caring, and clear communication in the previous steps. Now you and your partner get to play with ideas, to consider both fantastic and practical options, and to pool your creative energy by *brainstorming*. This creative approach to the problem will encourage you to break your stalemate by developing new ideas and options to reach a mutually satisfactory solution. You will also learn how to experiment and explore new possibilities to see if they might work.

Whether your problem is simple (dividing up housework) or complex (solving sexual problems or money worries), following the guidelines and techniques in this chapter will lead you to success.

Skills and Barriers in Exploring Options

Exploring Options means thinking of as many possible solutions to choose from as you can. The more choices you have, the more likely that a mutually satisfactory solution can be found. The skills you will learn to facilitate Exploring Options and deciding are:

* *The Abundance Worksheet,* which helps you overcome the fear that your problem cannot be solved by teaching you how to gain a deeper understanding of the dynamics underlying the problem, and look at it from a new, more creative perspective.

* *Brainstorming,* in which you creatively think of new options until you have enough to solve the problem.

* *Research and experimenting,* which help you gather more information when you can't figure out a mutually satisfactory solution.

* *Deciding,* a simple process of picking the best option out of several.

* *Confirming the decision,* which makes sure you have not overlooked any confusion or misunderstanding in your choice.

* *Celebration,* which acknowledges and confirms your successful decision, and creates confidence in your ability to solve problems and enthusiasm for the next negotiation.

* *Renegotiation,* which takes the pressure off your decision making by allowing you to accommodate unexpected outcomes or situation changes.

The barriers that are likely to get in the way of Exploring Options and Deciding are:

* *Apparent scarcity:* feeling anxious that the problem is unsolvable, which can tempt you to compete, power play, or rescue, thus preventing you from finding cooperative solution.

* *Hopelessness:* becoming overwhelmed by trying to solve all possible aspects, past, present, and future (which are

usually unforeseeable) of the problem now, which discourages both of you and makes creative thinking difficult.

* *Confusion:* misunderstanding or mistaking your agreement, which leads to thinking you have the problem solved when you don't.
* *Criticism:* stifling brainstorming by being critical of suggested ideas, which prevents you from freely suggesting new options, and limits the possible solutions to the problem.

If you are caught up in any of the above barriers, you may not see all the possible options (and therefore, not be able to make the best choice) because your anxiety about your differences will interfere with your creative thinking. In most cases, it is actually only the *perception* of the people involved that no possible mutually satisfactory solution can be found, or that someone's wants will have to go unsatisfied, or that the problem is impossible to solve.

If you do get stuck in what seems to be an impossible problem, instead of letting your fears push you into competing and arguing, you can recognize that it is just an *apparent scarcity,* and use the Abundance Worksheet in this chapter to examine your deeper wants and expand your boundaries to end the stalemate. You will probably find that there are plenty of workable options, and a mutually beneficial solution can be found. Don and Dale used the abundance worksheet to break their power struggle and find out what lay behind each of their wants for an office, so each of them could understand the other better, feel less afraid of being unsatisfied, and work together to find a mutual solution.

Hopelessness can be overcome by a *research project or experiment.* If even the Abundance Worksheet doesn't help, and you feel that you will never find a way to solve your problem, you probably don't have enough information. Setting up a research project to gather more facts or an experiment to see which possible solutions might work will reassure you that a solution is possible, and give you the extra knowledge you need to find one. *When Joe wasn't sure that having a housekeeper would work for him, he and Carol experimented with a housecleaning service on a trial basis before making their final decision.*

Even after you've reached a decision, it's possible for one or both of you to be confused or to differ in your understanding of what the decision is, so *confirming the decision* is a skill that helps you verify that you both know what solution you've agreed to. *Joe and Carol found that confirming their decision by writing it down eliminated their confusion.*

Finally, even the best of solutions may not be workable forever because situations and people change, so *renegotiation* will help you be flexible and able to adapt to change, and make finding a working solution less overwhelming. Being able to renegotiate at any time means you don't have to be able to predict what might happen in the future in order to reach a decision today, because you can renegotiate if the situation changes.

Once you've reached a successful decision, *celebrating* your success helps you acknowledge what you have accomplished, put a clear and positive end to the negotiation, increase your warmth and goodwill, and reward yourselves for work well done.

When you have explored options through the Abundance Worksheet and brainstorming, made your decision, confirmed it and celebrated, your cooperative negotiation is complete, and you and your partner will have the satisfaction of successful teamwork, mutual support, and a mutually satisfying result.

Brainstorming

If the solution isn't obvious as soon as you both know each other's wants, it is necessary to create new ideas, until you find one that solves the problem to your mutual satisfaction. But old, habitual thinking can block creativity and make developing new options difficult. These old habits include:

* *Rigid or limited ideas* ("shoulds"). The belief that you can only do things in old, familiar ways (such as the way your family did it), can prevent you from considering new and better options.
* *Criticism*, which can stifle new ideas before they are even fully formed.

    * *Old ingrained thinking habits,* which can prevent you
      from seeing possible solutions because they are unfamiliar.

If you're having difficulty creating a mutually satisfactory solution, you can stir your creative imagination by learning to *brainstorm.* Brainstorming, a favorite technique of innovative companies such as Microsoft, was created to overcome limitations on creativity. The object is to develop a list of random ideas without limiting them by practical considerations. Among a long list of wild ideas, you'll find some that are fresh and feasible to choose from. Brainstorming will help you and your partner free up your thinking and explore options.

Your creativity is limited when you:

    * See a problem only one way.
    * Are so accustomed to a particular way of doing things
      that new ideas don't occur to you.
    * Approach problem-solving with a perfectionist, hopeless,
      or critical attitude.
    * Have been taught by your family or society that certain
      options are unthinkable (you "shouldn't" do it).
    * Don't have enough information.

Learning to brainstorm shows you how to overcome the criticism that can block your creative ideas by getting playful and energetic, and allowing even silly or impossible ideas to be part of the process. By not considering the reasonableness of options until after brainstorming, you give your creativity free reign. Brainstorming breaks through old, familiar concepts and stimulates new, more creative ideas by creating conditions (moving around physically, writing large, setting a time limit, being playful, and stating rapid-fire, excited suggestions) that encourage a non-critical, unrestricted, free flow of ideas. As you brainstorm, you and your partner learn to move around to loosen yourselves up, freely generate ideas you haven't thought of before, write them down, review them, evaluate them, and choose the best solution. You'll break through the limits of your previous thinking by getting outrageous, silly, creative, and inventive. By having fun and energizing each other, you'll find innovative solutions spontaneously arise, even when the problems seem unsolvable. When you allow the silly ideas such as "my fairy godmother will come and fix it," or "I'll win the lottery" to be okay, you won't stifle the new, *reasonable* idea that may just be perfect to solve your problem. When your thinking is restricted, the following exercise will show you how to loosen it up, generate new ideas, and remove the limitations that normally would inhibit the flow. It will also help you decide if you need further information or research.

Exercise: Brainstorming

In this exercise, you will make a list of as many different ideas as you possibly can, as quickly as you can. It is important to write down every idea, whether or not it seems to make sense, be possible, or be reasonable. If you eliminate ideas because they are not reasonable, practical, sensible, or acceptable at this point, you will block the flow of new ideas and stifle your creativity. You can tell your thinking is not restricted when you have as many silly ideas as usable ones.

Choose a place where you won't be interrupted, and allow 20 to 45 minutes depending on the difficulty of the problem. Have a large pad, piece of paper, chalkboard, or marking board and crayons, chalk, or markers for writing your ideas because physically moving around helps you to stay loose and energized.

1. **Write the problem down.** *Write down the problem in terms of each of your basic wants so that it is in plain sight while you brainstorm. Having it in front of you will be a constant reminder of the reason you are trying to generate the options, and it will help you stay on track. If you have trouble clarifying the problem, follow the steps in the Your Adult Wants Exercise (Chapter 5).*

Don and Dale wrote: We both want the back bedroom for an office, and there's not enough room for both of us.

Paul and Mary, negotiating their vacation wants, wrote: How to have a vacation in mountainous pine forest and sun on a beach, too.

For Carol and Joe, the statement read: How to take the burden of housework off Carol without putting it on Joe.

2. Write as many ideas as you can in 10 minutes. *Take turns writing your ideas on the board or pad as you come up with them, to keep you moving, and raise the energy level. Set a timer for 10 minutes. During that time, each of you should try to contribute as many ideas as you can, calling them out and writing them down. Saying your ideas out loud as well as writing them creates a playful atmosphere, reminiscent of a game of charades or a TV game show. Be silly, be boisterous, shout ideas out, don't worry about being sensible or reasonable, and let the energy build as it does on a TV game show. The first ideas may be hesitant, but as you get into the "game" and begin to toss ideas back and forth, your energy will rise. The more your energy flows, the more your ideas will flow. Don't criticize or comment on the ideas. You can evaluate each other's ideas later.*

Paul and Mary's session went like this:

Mary: (playful) *Cut down a tree and take it to the beach!*

Paul: (joining in) *I know—play Russian roulette, and the winner goes to Rio on the life insurance!*

Mary: *Separate vacations!*

Paul: *We'll split our time in half—one week at the beach, one week in the mountains!*

Mary: *Alternate days by helicopter!*

Paul: *Double our vacation time this year and do two weeks at each place!*

Mary: (suddenly inspired) *Wait! How about a mountain lake?*

Paul: (enthused) *Lake Tahoe!*

Mary: (more ideas) *Pine Mountain Lake!*

While Don and Dale were slightly more serious:

Don: (starting serious, getting lighter) *You take the back bedroom, I'll take the master bedroom and we'll sleep in the backyard.*

Dale: (thinking) *You take space in one of those "executive suites" with a receptionist.*

Don: *Put Kendra in day care and you rent an office so I can have the back bedroom.*

Dale: (having fun) *Let's flip a coin to decide and go to the beach right now.*

Don: *I take a salaried job instead of working for myself.*

Dale: (doesn't mean it) *I'll take a salaried job and you work at home and take care of Kendra.*

Don: *Get real successful at our businesses, so we can have more money and buy a bigger place.*

Dale: (wild idea) *Rob a bank.*

Don: *Whoever has the bedroom office takes care of Kendra.*

Dale: *Use the living room for your office, and I can use the back bedroom.*

Don: (inspired) *Maybe I could find a low-rent office and sublet some of it to cover the rent.*

Dale: (enthused) *Maybe Tom and Julie would want to share it with you.*

Don: *Let's keep it the way it is while we research the low-rent office suite idea and see if someone wants to sublet from me. If that works, and I get free or low cost office space, I'd be happy to let you have the bedroom.*

3. **When your 10 minutes are up, review your list.** *Enjoy the wild or silly suggestions (such as "fly by helicopter" or "Rob a bank"). Each of you underlines the ones that work for you. If there are options that you both like, pick the one you agree is best and proceed to clarify and confirm your decision as discussed on page 215.*

Paul and Mary instantly agreed on a mountain lake, now they only have to decide which one.

When Don and Dale review their suggestions, four of them stand out as feasible:

1. Get real successful at our businesses, so we can have more money and buy a bigger place.

2. Find a low-rent office suite and sublet some of it to cover the rent.

3. Find someone to share the outside office rent with Don.

4. Keep things the way they are while we research the low-rent office suite idea and see if someone wants to share rent. If that works, and I get free or low office rent, I'd be happy to let you have the bedroom.

4. If there is no idea that's good enough, follow Steps 1-3 again. *You may need to do several 10-minute brainstorming sessions to loosen up and get the creativity flowing and reach a solution that works for both of you. Remember: The more fun you have, the more creative you'll be, but do attempt to stay focused on addressing the problem.*

Brainstorming almost always works. When you get creative about your solutions, the obvious ones usually show up, as they did with Paul and Mary. When the solution isn't obvious, you will need to be creative in searching for options that satisfy both your wants.

Paul and Mary's vacation dilemma was solved by going to a mountain lake that had a beach.

Fred and Naomi discovered, after some intimate conversation and creative negotiation, some acceptable and mutually enjoyable ways Fred could "seduce" Naomi, and also ways to take the pressure off Naomi: For example, Naomi could hold Fred while he satisfied himself with masturbation, and they could watch erotic movies, or have one-sided sex where Naomi helped Fred.

Don and Dale came up with a number of acceptable ideas, which they will explore in this chapter.

Carol and Joe resolved their problem by bringing in a cleaning service every two weeks and starting a savings fund for a dishwasher.

Apparent Scarcity

If, after brainstorming, you or your partner is still having trouble Stating and Exploring Wants, the problem may be an *apparent scarcity.* One or both of you may have gotten caught up in the perception that there is no possible solution because there isn't enough of something (time, money, love, patience, food, goodwill, space, energy) to go around for both of you to get what you want. That is an "apparent" scarcity because the scarcity only appears real. The vast majority of the time, scarcity is imagined, and what appears to be a scarcity is actually created with a competitive attitude. The scarcity almost always disappears when carefully examined in terms of what the partners really want. Most couples are convinced that there is a scarcity (someone's going to be dissatisfied) before they even see whether at least one satisfactory solution can be found.

> **In Don and Dale's first attempt at discussion, they began by stating wants, but soon became anxious, competitive, and got distracted from the problem of how to redistribute house and office space. There was no mutually agreeable solution, because they never tried to find one.**

When you fear not getting your wants and needs met, your natural reaction is to defend your "share" and compete for what you want. When this happens, you are less able to hear your partner's wants, or to state your own calmly and without exaggeration. This competition can create the very scarcity you fear by causing you to miss many of the possible options, which is what happened with Don and Dale. Their anxiety prevented them from seeing any options in their first discussion, but they came up with many when they overcame their fear of scarcity with brainstorming.

Overcoming Apparent Scarcity

The perception of scarcity arises from false limits placed on the problem. Believing you can't both have what you want prevents you from considering all the possibilities. Creating abundance depends on expanding these limits. This can be done in two ways:

1. *Examine your wants.* You can come up with an "instant idea" of what you want, without stopping to think about why you want it, or whether it will really satisfy you. Often this idea is a possible solution that might satisfy a want, rather than the want itself.

For Don, using the back bedroom for his office was his solution for saving on overhead and feeling isolated alone in his office. His actual, underlying wants were to save money and have some company, but he passed over them and came up with a possible solution, which he presented to Dale as his want. To Dale it felt like a preemptive decision, limiting Dale's options.

When your wants are in conflict with your partner's, and you can't find an option that will satisfy you both, taking time to examine exactly what you want, why you want it, and whether there are any other options, can help you break through some of the limits and reach a mutually satisfying solution.

2. *Expand your boundaries.* Expanding the boundaries means becoming aware of artificial limitations, false ideas, or family and cultural taboos (that you "shouldn't" or "can't" do it) that keep you from considering options that would resolve your apparent scarcity.

Don had settled on the back bedroom as the only solution, but when he realized he was limiting his options, he discovered many possibilities (saving to put an addition on the house, sharing a rented office suite, renting a mobile home and parking it in the driveway, making the dining room into his office so Dale could use the back bedroom, or converting part of the garage).

Naomi and Fred, who are having sexual problems, believe there is scarcity in their relationship. Fred is dissatisfied with the frequency and availability of sexual relations with Naomi, and Naomi feels a lack of cuddling and affection. When they explored their options,

> Fred discovered that paying a little extra affectionate attention (holding hands, hugging, casual touching during the day, sitting close while watching TV) to Naomi got her interested in being sexual with him much more often, and Naomi discovered that when she wasn't feeling as sexual as Fred, he was satisfied with masturbating while she held him, or watching erotic movies together, as long as she was happy, too.

Often you lack options because you are only looking in one place or one moment for the solution to your problem. When we did this exercise in workshops, we found that if we gave a group of 10 people three or four grapes and told them "there is enough to go around" they tended to focus on how 10 people might share four grapes, never noticing that there were several pounds of grapes out in the open, close by. Even though we said nothing about being limited to the grapes we handed them, they automatically limited their boundaries to what they were given. Most of them said they "didn't think to look around" or "thought they shouldn't ask for more grapes" although there were no such rules.

> Similarly, although neither Joe nor Carol want to do housework, they don't consider bringing in a cleaning service to do it, so they have an apparent scarcity (of someone who is willing to do it).

You or your partner may think you have to have a solution "right now" when you actually have a few days or weeks, and in that extra time, you can easily find a mutually satisfactory option. If, after both of you have stated your wants, you have tried brainstorming but you're still competing, the following exercise will help you break out of limited thinking, expand your boundaries and discover new options. Although it is easier to think of options for some problems (how to get the car fixed) than for others (a sexual problem, or caring for an aged parent); any time you feel that the problem is unsolvable, or feel helpless or hopeless about it, you are probably dealing with an apparent scarcity. When you use the Abundance Worksheet, you'll discover that a solution is probably possible, and feel reassured, more hopeful, and able to think more clearly.

Exercise: The Abundance Worksheet

The Abundance Worksheet is a tool you and your partner can use to get you moving again when you are stuck in an apparent scarcity due to a conflict between your wants. We've shown you how Don and Dale did each step as an example to follow.

Step 1. Describe the apparent scarcity. *The purpose of this step is to state your wants, where you disagree, and what the limits seem to be. List both partners' wants, arguments, explanations, and rationalizations of why you want what you want, and the limits you envision running into, all together. Then, pare down your original description until you can develop a "summary" sentence or two that states the problem as simply as possible.*

Dale wants back bedroom for office. Don wants it, too. Limited rooms available. Work at home saves childcare expense and is better for child. Eliminate travel time and expense to work, wear on car. Save cost of office rent. Amount of space needed. We both need offices. Summary: We both want the back bedroom for an office, and there's not enough room for both of us.

Step 2. Explore your wants. *The purpose of this step is to delve more deeply into what you want, and to try and discover the wants* behind *your stated wants. It's okay to include what you* don't *want, because as you have seen in the previous exercise, you can turn your "don't wants" around and they become wants. Do this by asking yourself the following questions:*

* "*Why* do I want what I've stated as my wants? "
* "What would having it accomplish, change, or solve for me?"
* "What about the current situation makes me dissatisfied or unhappy, and how will getting what I want solve it?"

Once you have answered these questions, you'll be able to write a list of what you want, ending with what your ideal option is.

Here is Don and Dale's:

Don's Wants	Dale's Wants
I want the back bedroom for an office because:	*I want the back bedroom for an office because:*
I need to reduce my overhead.	*I want a light-filled room to work in (dining room is too dark).*
I hate commuting.	
I don't like being isolated at my current office.	*I want to be able to watch Kendra in the backyard.*
I want equal rights and equal opportunities in this relationship. It's my house, too.	*I don't want to spend extra rent for an office.*
What I really want is to have the money to have an office suite near home to share with others.	*What I really want is to work at home to be with Kendra, and the back bedroom would make the best office.*

Continue asking yourself the questions, and expanding your lists, until you feel you have gotten down to your most basic wants and options about the issue. Then share your lists. As you explore your underlying, more detailed wants in this step, enough new options should become clear to you that your apparent scarcity disappears, and you can go on to Exploring options and Deciding.

Don and Dale learned a lot about themselves and each other by exploring what they wanted, and the problems became less threatening, because they could see the reasons behind the wants, and understand each other's positions better. But they didn't feel that the apparent scarcity was completely gone. *If exploring wants does not give you enough information, go on to the next step.*

Step 3. Expand the boundaries of the problem. *The purpose of this step is to help you remove arbitrary and previously unnoticed restrictions or false limits you may have placed on the possible solutions to your problem. Answer the following questions as they relate to your apparent scarcity:*

Is there anything you have not considered doing, having, saying, or trying, because you don't think it's worth mentioning?

How can you stretch your view of what's possible and what your resources are?

Can you include more space, more time, other people, money you weren't thinking of before?

Are there any "shoulds" you don't really need to obey?

What are the limitations you are placing on the situation?

For Don and Dale, looking beyond the boundary of the back bedroom produced the following options:

1. Use the dining room.

2. Convert the garage.

3. Use the attic or the basement.

4. Add a room.

5. Get a motor home and set it up in the yard.

6. Get a tent and set it up in the yard.

7. Move to a larger house.

8. Rent space nearby.

9. Reorganize the house, move our bedroom into the dining room, eat in the kitchen, and use both bedrooms for office space.

10. Both squeeze into the back bedroom, and pay Don's office rent into a building fund.

11. Whoever gets the bedroom shares the cost for the other to rent an office outside the house.

In exploring their wants and expanding their boundaries, the partners learned a lot about each other and themselves, and can now see that a solution is not as impossible as they previously thought. Don and Dale have so many new and promising options that their problem should be quite easy to solve now.

Fred and Naomi's problem, being intangible and emotional, and involving sex—an issue which is difficult for many people to talk frankly about—could be more difficult to solve than Don and

Dale's more mundane and concrete issue. But when they explored their wants and expanded their boundaries, they came up with the following ideas:

* Sex doesn't always have to be the same for both of us. Fred could masturbate, and Naomi could just hold him as he does.

* We could cuddle and watch erotic movies, so Fred can feel sexy, and Naomi can get affection.

* Affection can include holding hands, talking quietly, sending flowers.

* Naomi can ask Fred for whatever would make her feel safe whenever he makes a sexual overture.

* Fred and Naomi could go for sex therapy and find out more options.

After expanding your boundaries and exploring options, you may discover that you still have doubts or questions, which indicates that you don't have enough information to really solve the problem (what are the legal issues? how will it feel to do something new? can we really live up to our agreement?). If that is the case, then setting up a *research* project will help you find the answers.

Doing Research

Usually, when you have found an option you both like, it is easy to move forward to a decision to implement it to solve your problem. There are times, however, when an *immediate* solution isn't obvious, because more information is needed. Sometimes one or both of you may not be certain about whether or not the option you have selected is the right one. For example:

* You may come up with a good idea, but you don't know if it will really work until you gather more facts.
* You may come up with an idea that you *think* will work, but you won't know until you try it.
* One partner may be delighted with an idea, but the other won't be sure until he or she sees what it's really like.

When this happens, you need to research either by gathering information or trying out your solution on a temporary basis.

Experimentation: Try It out Temporarily

The only way to find out if some solutions (such as who does a particular household chore, how to handle a problem with your families, a new sexual variation, or changing the arrangement of your living room) will work is to try them, on an experimental basis. When you and your partner *think* you have a solution, but you're not sure if it will work, or one of you feels unsatisfied with it, you can try it out on an experimental basis. This way, you can see how well it works before committing to an agreement.

Testing a possible solution gives a chance to gather information from a trial run. By trying a solution for a limited period of time, you can find out if it actually works and if it is mutually satisfactory. The Guidelines for Doing Research will show you how. In order to have enough information to decide on a mutually satisfactory solution you may also need to gather information.

Gathering Information

If, when you have considered options, you find you have a lot of unanswered questions (how much will it cost? how long will it take? do we know enough to do it ourselves, or should we hire someone?) and need more facts to know if a proposed solution is feasible, you can research by gathering information. Gathering information means to check with resources (look it up in the library, search the Internet, take a class or workshop, call businesses in the yellow pages, ask a lawyer, a doctor, a plumber, a travel agent, a mechanic, or other expert, or ask friends or business associates who have experience) to get more facts and details about the situation.

When you agree to do information research, you temporarily put your problem-solving on hold, divide up the research chores, and set a time to get back together and share what you've learned, to see if your chosen option is indeed feasible.

Guidelines: Doing Research

In the rare cases when brainstorming and the Abundance Worksheet don't lead to a solution, there may not be an immediate or obvious solution available that will satisfy both of you. You and your partner may be uncertain whether your options will work because you don't know everything you need to evaluate them. In that case, you will want to use these guidelines to initiate a formal research project.

1. Agree to research. *If you have a possible solution, but you have questions about how it will work, agree to research in the same way you reached an Agreement to Negotiate. It is helpful if you reassure each other by stating out loud that the purpose of the research is to get more information that will help both of you get your wants met. If you don't agree that research is a good idea at this point, use your communication skills (Active Listening, Attentive Speaking, and "I" messages) to find out why. If your partner is worried about something, reassure him or her by using the Guidelines for Reassurance (page 113).*

2. Choose the type of research. *Choose either:*

A. Experimentation: *To experiment, pick one of your possible solutions to try out for a limited period of time to see how it works, as* Joe and Carol did when they hired a housekeeper on a trial basis for a month. *You can agree to try one or two different options on a trial basis. If you choose this option, you'll use the steps in Part 1.*

B. Information Gathering: *Seeking out more facts and details about the solution, until you know how it works.* Paul and Mary found out more about traveling by splitting the work: Paul called travel agents to see what places that have mountains and lakes with beaches are available, and Mary went to the library to look at travel magazines and books on vacation ideas. They talked to friends and read the travel ads in the Sunday paper together. *If you choose this option, you'll use the steps in Part 2.*

Once you have agreed on the kind of research, use the following steps: Part 1 if you've decided to experiment, and Part 2 if you've decided to gather more information.

Part 1. If You Decide to Experiment:

1. Set a time limit. *Set an estimated time for how long you'll try your experiment* (Carol and Joe decided on one month) *before discussing the results. Limiting the time for the trial will reassure both of you that you haven't yet committed to a final decision, and it will reassure both of you that you'll complete the negotiation.*

2. Set time and place. *Set another meeting date (in accordance with Step 1.) when you can discuss how the trial went and whether the solution works or not. This provides the uninterrupted, unhurried time you need to discuss the results of your experiment, and complete your negotiation.*

3. Conduct the experiment. *Try your temporary solution for the specified time, with both of you observing how well you think it works. This trial period will give you the experience you need to know if your solution is mutually satisfying. You may want to make notes you can use in your discussion later. In the notes, include how well you liked or didn't like it, and what you learned from it. This will make it easier to communicate what you learn.* Joe and Carol met after the housekeeper had been there several times, and Joe decided the housekeeping solution was fine with him. There was no privacy problem because he wasn't home during that time. Carol loved the extra help, and was less tired after work, so she was more pleasant for Joe to be around, and they both decided the expense was well worth it, so they agreed that their problem was solved. *If the trial had not solved their problem, they would have resumed brainstorming, using the new information they had from having tried the housekeeper.*

4. Resume negotiation. *After the trial period, meet at the specified time and place, and discuss the information you gained from your experiment. If your trial experiment seems to satisfy both of you, your problem is solved. If it doesn't work, resume Exploring Options and continue on through the Negotiation Tree.*

Part 2. If You Decide To Gather Information:

1. Divide the work. *Decide what information you need* (Paul and Mary needed to know about cost of resorts, what resorts were in the mountains with lakes nearby, travel costs and accommodations) *and where it is available* (travel agents, the travel section of the paper, the Internet, friends) *and divide up the work. For example, one of you contacts half of the sources, the other contacts the rest.*

2. Set time and place. *Set another meeting date to discuss what you've learned, and how it affects your options. This will ensure that you resume negotiation when you've gathered all the facts, and also puts a time limit on how long you have to complete your research.*

3. Gather information. *Do the research you agreed on, take notes, gather pamphlets, articles, facts and figures as needed, and summarize what you've found out so that you can explain it to your partner.* Paul and Mary brought newspaper articles, brochures, and lists of prices to their meeting.

4. Resume negotiation. *Meet as agreed to discuss the information you gathered. Most likely, the new facts will clarify your options, and you can agree on a solution to your problem. If not, you may want to try an experiment or return to brainstorming.*

Decide and Confirm Your Decision

Once you come up with a mutual solution, you may feel that your negotiation has been successful, and the process is complete: but there is one more crucial step.

If you quit the process here, you might unwittingly create three problems:

1. One of you may not really be in full agreement because you feel the agreement places some undue burden on you, but you haven't let your reservations be known. This is our old friend, the rescue, coming up one last time, and causing you to not want to disappoint the partner who is excited about the option. As always, rescuing builds resentment, and you could find that the agreement you thought you

made doesn't really work. *When Don and Dale discussed their new office situation, Don noticed he felt a little burdened and resentful, but he didn't say anything because their negotiation had taken quite a long time, and he thought Dale might be upset if he objected. So, when the time came to move the offices, Don felt angry and was irritable and uncooperative.*

2.   You and you partner may understand the agreement differently and not realize it because you haven't restated it clearly, and inadvertently create different hidden expectations that will erupt later. *When Joe and Carol decided to try a housekeeper, they created some confusion:*

Joe: *Okay, here's the agreement: We hire a housekeeper for a one-month trial period. See if we can get someone for $60 a day. Then we'll meet the first Saturday after the month is up and decide if we like it.*

Carol: *Good, I'll look for a housekeeper.*

Carol did find one who charged $60 a day, and signed up for every Wednesday for one month. It wasn't until the fourth cleaning day that Joe realized she was coming weekly, when he thought she was going to come twice a month. He was dismayed to discover his cost was twice what he thought it was.

3.   You both may not feel equally satisfied and not realize it because you haven't been clear about what is expected from each of you and what each of you expects to get from the agreement, which can lead to one partner unconsciously sabotaging or not living up to the agreement. *Paul got really enthused about their vacation in the mountains, and decided on a small, rustic lakeside resort in Washington state. Mary agreed at first, but later began to realize that the resort was not nearly as luxurious as she wanted, and she started complaining about something every time Paul mentioned the trip: the packing was difficult, the airline food would be lousy, who would care for the cat while they were away.*

Mary's disappointment was causing her to unconsciously sabotage their plans.

To avoid these problems, you must be certain that you are both in agreement about the solution, that you and your partner understand your agreement in the same way, and that you are both equally satisfied. To ensure that this is the case you will need to formally decide on a solution, confirm and then finalize your decision.

Decide

If you have laid the proper groundwork by exploring options until you have several good ones to choose from, brainstorming if you don't have enough, and experimenting or gathering information if you need more facts, deciding is usually very straightforward. Once you have enough possible solutions for the problem, at least one acceptable solution will stand out to each of you. If you have not done enough preliminary work, you will not have enough options, or one or both of you will feel dissatisfied with what you have. In that case, you need to go back (as the Negotiation Tree tells you) and repeat an earlier step: the abundance worksheet, brainstorming, or a research project. Sometimes one partner will simply be unwilling to make a decision. In that case, you need to solve the problem for yourself, as in the guidelines in Chapter 3 (page 146).

You can tell that you have selected a mutually satisfying decision because you will feel a sense of completion or relief as the tension of disagreeing is resolved. *When Joe and Carol had completed their decision about housework, Carol noticed a feeling of relief, a relaxation of tension, when she thought she wouldn't have to deal with housecleaning and in addition, she had Joe's support and approval for the solution. Joe felt relieved, too. Without realizing it, he had felt pressured and guilty about not wanting to do his share. Being cooperative and honest about their wants, and successful at finding a viable, mutually satisfying solution was gratifying and they both felt full of goodwill and celebration.*

If you both feel relieved, enthusiastic, or satisfied when you have come to your decision, you are ready to finalize your agreement. Follow these simple guidelines for deciding once you have enough options.

Guidelines: Deciding

Step 1. Choose your individual favorite. *From the options that you've developed on your abundance worksheet, through the Brainstorming Exercise, or through a research project, each of you separately choose the option or options you feel satisfies your wants. (If you do not have an option that satisfies you, do the Brainstorming Exercise again, or begin a research project to get more information.)*

Step 2. Share your choices. *Tell each other what your favorite choice is. If you've chosen the same one, your decision is made, and you can go onto Confirming the Decision. If you choose different options, continue onto Step 3.*

Step 3. Try to combine choices. *Try to combine your favorite choices into one option that covers both of them. You can use your brainstorming techniques or the Abundance Worksheet to generate the new, combined idea.* Once Paul and Mary agreed on a mountain resort by a lake, Paul wanted a rustic resort, but Mary's choice was a more luxurious one. They found out they could combine those choices by choosing a resort in a wildlife preserve that had all the amenities of a fine hotel, including a lake and a pool, but had hiking, backpacking and fishing also available. *When you believe you have found a suitable combination, continue onto Step 4.*

Step 4. Check for relief. *Check with each other to see how you feel about the decision. Once your decision is made, you should both feel somewhat relieved, relaxed, and satisfied. If you do, your decision is made, and you can go on to Confirm the Decision. If you don't feel relieved or complete about your decision, mentally review your response to the proposed solution. Does something feel ignored or unfinished? Do you seem to have vague objections or doubts about it? If so, your decision is still not complete, and you need to brainstorm. Use the Abundance Worksheet, or set up a research project to generate more information.*

When Don and Dale discussed their new office situation, Don noticed he felt a little burdened and resentful, and he realized

*their decision meant he was agreeing to a lot of work and respon-
sibility so that he could have a new outside office. He discussed
his reservations with Dale. As a result, they modified their decision to give Dale more of the setup work. At that point, the
agreement felt much more equal to Don, and he felt relieved
and happy to make the decision. Dale still felt he was getting
what he wanted and was happy to make the adjustment.*

If, like Don, you feel uneasy, confused, or unsure, you may:

* Discuss your misgivings with your partner.

** Review the decision for flaws or omissions, and go back to brain-
storming to develop more options or fine-tune the ones you have.*

** Decide to experiment with your decision to see if it works well.
If you are experiencing some doubt and cannot figure out what it
is, turn your best options into an experiment, using the guidelines for doing research.*

Confirming the Decision

Once you have selected and agreed on an option, it is still necessary
to make a formal agreement confirming your choice to be sure that both
of you understand the solution, agree to it, and interpret it the same way.
To Confirm the Decision, you review the decision separately and communicate it verbally or in writing. Skipping this important step could
lead you to create a *hidden expectation*, because you may find out later
that each of you understood the agreement differently. *Joe and Carol
were shocked to find out that they hadn't understood how much the
housekeeper would cost.* Following these guidelines will prevent such
confusion.

Guidelines: Confirming Your Decision

1. Repeat the decision. *In your own words, express your understanding of the decision you have reached. This is a verbal "run-
through" or practice of your agreement, which allows you to make
sure you've covered all the details, as well as a chance to imagine
together how satisfactory your solution will be. Each of you should*

share your understanding of what the solution is, and how it will work. When Joe and Carol reconfirmed their decision about housework to clear up the confusion, Joe said: "As I understand it, we'll hire the housekeeper to come every other week, and we'll split the cost." Carol agreed. *Your discussion should also cover what you expect to contribute to the solution.* Joe and Carol would each pay half the cost. *And how you will benefit from the solution.* Joe and Carol both have a clean house, Carol will be less stressed, and Joe won't have to do housework.

2. Finalize your agreement. *Once you both have confirmed your decision, you need to make a formal agreement, like a contract. State your agreement out loud.* Because they settled for a verbal agreement, Joe and Carol created confusion, so this time they decided to write out their contract. Carefully written out, Joe and Carol's new contract read: "We will hire the housekeeper to come one day every other week, for a one month trial period, at a cost of no more than $50 each time." *Verbal agreements can leave room for misunderstandings like Joe and Carol's, if you skip important details. The next step guards against such problems.*

3. Write out what you confirmed. *When Cooperative Problem Solving is new to you, or when your decision is complex, we recommend you avoid possible disagreement or unhappiness later by writing up a formal agreement that lists what you both feel you have decided on. Using what you confirmed in the last set of guidelines, finalize your decision by writing it out in contract form, stating what each of you expects to contribute to and to gain from the agreement, as in these examples:*

Don and Dale's written contract read: "Don will temporarily move his office into the dining room to save money and Dale will move his into the back bedroom. They will both ask friends to see who would like to share an outside office rental with Don. Don will look for suitable office space to rent, and Dale will share the moving expenses and renovation work (painting, shelves, moving furniture, installing phones, etc.) for Don to move into the house and back out again later. When enough money is saved, Don will move into his shared office with friends, and Dale will still have his office in the back bedroom."

John and Rose's contract read: "Rose will go back to school with John's full encouragement and support. Rose will continue to support John with executive dinners and parties and running errands when necessary, and John agrees to give her enough notice and to accommodate her school schedule (no surprise dinner guests the night before a test)."

Writing down your agreement minimizes problems by revealing any obvious areas of misunderstanding about your decision and by forcing you to be clearer and more precise about the specifics of your agreement. This ensures that you both understand exactly what the agreement is, and if you get confused later, you can check your written agreement to clear up the confusion.

Once you become familiar with Cooperative Problem Solving, you will usually find it sufficient to confirm their decision verbally, in a few words informally stated. But when a problem is complex or long-standing, a written contract is always helpful in making sure your agreement is clear.

4. Read and agree. *Read your written agreement out loud, and let each other know you've agreed to it. Once you've done this, your agreement is finalized, unless circumstances change.*

Even when you both feel sure your solution is perfect, circumstances may change, requiring a change in your solution. *If Don were offered an excellent job, he might give up his business, making an office unnecessary, or if someone fell ill in Mary's family, and she and Paul decided to use their vacation to help out, their vacation plans would be shelved.*

For that reason, in Cooperative Problem Solving you need to both note as part of your agreement that all solutions need to be renegotiable at any time.

Renegotiation

To honor your commitment to each other's satisfaction, any solution must be renegotiable if either of you becomes unhappy with it. No couple can foresee all possible events, and any solution that works in the situation you have today may be obsolete when something different happens tomorrow. As you grow older, like Rose and John, your external circumstances may change (retirement, grown children, new interests) or, you may get more successful (Don and Dale eventually had thriving businesses, and a whole suite of offices), or problems may arise (illness, reduction of income, an acquired handicap), or you may just grow tired of the way you are doing things.

Cooperating means working together to find new solutions if old solutions no longer work for one or both of you. Because none of us can predict the future, it is impossible to find solutions that will cover all these eventualities. Trying to find the "perfect solution" makes a solution seem impossible, and can create pressure and anxiety which can bring back old competitive behavior. *Don and Dale were well along in carrying out their agreement when Don found out that one of his co-renters dropped out and another wanted to delay moving in for six more weeks, which made the rent too expensive. Don asked Dale to negotiate a modification in their time schedule (which would also affect their financial agreement), and they were able to renegotiate a six-week extension to the original plan.*

Guidelines for Successful Renegotiation

1. Be renegotiable. *Begin by adding the phrase "all solutions are renegotiable at any time" to all your agreements. This removes the pressure to make the solution "perfect" for all possible outcomes, and reassures both of you that you can always renegotiate.*

2. Renegotiate, don't break agreements. *If you can break an agreement anytime it becomes inconvenient or unpleasant for you, your partner will never be able to trust any of your agreements; and vice versa. Renegotiating before you break an agreement makes sure no one is surprised, betrayed or deceived, and enhances the trust between you.*

3. Ask for renegotiation. *Just as you did in agreeing to negotiate, let your partner know that your previous solution isn't working for you, and why, and formally request a renegotiation.*

4. Have a plan for emergencies. *If an emergency occurs (my car caught fire on a business trip, you weren't home when I called) and you are forced to break an agreement (I had to spend the money we were saving for our vacation to fix the car) without renegotiating, formally acknowledge that you did it, explain why it was an emergency, and apologize, then renegotiate the original agreement to cover such emergencies.*

5. Renegotiateslight changes. *If you are only seeking to modify your agreement slightly, your renegotiation may be as simple as setting the stage and considering other options.* Paul and Mary agreed on Lake Tahoe for their vacation, but Paul later became concerned about the cost and wanted to consider reducing expenses. They decided on a less expensive hotel in a few minutes.

6. For big changes, begin at the beginning. *If the agreement you want to renegotiate is a basic or long-standing one, you may need to follow the Negotiation Tree from the beginning.* When John's retirement became imminent, he and Rose spent considerable time and care in negotiating their new arrangement to accommodate his retirement to Rose's new career.

The Cooperative Problem Solving process doesn't end with formalizing your decision. Instead, completing your negotiation takes another, and equally vital, step: to celebrate what you have both accomplished by working together to solve your problem. As a Free Couple, your goal is for Cooperative Problem Solving to become a natural way for the two of you to interact, so you will eventually welcome each opportunity to solve problems as a cooperative team. With practice, each of the steps of the Negotiation Tree will become easier until they seem natural to you, and you won't have to give it very much thought. Every negotiation will then be successful, and an opportunity for a celebration.

Celebration

Celebrating the successful completion of your Cooperative negotiation accomplishes many things:

* Celebration acknowledges and establishes in your minds that you've accomplished a satisfying end to what may have been a difficult problem.
* Celebration helps you focus on the good feelings you have about each other.
* Celebration produces what psychologists call a sense of "closure": a clear concluding moment, a feeling of resolution to your diligent work, so that there are no residual, unresolved thoughts or feelings with you as you proceed to your next task.
* Celebration makes you focus attention on the positive result of your negotiation, when most people tend to put most of their energy on the negative.
* Celebration provides a moment of warmth and goodwill, the hallmarks of freedom in your relationship.
* Celebration is a reward for work well done, and also creates motivation for future cooperative negotiation.

Most people have a tendency to give more attention to what *doesn't work* than what *does* work and so they never give themselves a chance to acknowledge and savor success. If you do this, you gain no sense of your accomplishments, and only become aware of what you feel you can't do. You then see yourselves as failures, your relationship as a struggle, and you can become discouraged enough to give up. The more difficult the problem you just solved, the greater the tendency to see negotiation as hard work, and so the more important it is to counteract that by celebrating.

If you neglect to celebrate the completion of your Cooperative Problem Solving, you will not be as motivated to begin on the next problem that needs to be solved. On the other hand, when you take the time to celebrate a successful negotiation, you allow yourselves to notice the good things about yourselves and your capacity for accomplishment. While a good cooperative solution is a reward in itself, giving yourselves an extra celebration of your success helps you realize how productive you can be as a couple, affirms the power of your teamwork, and acknowledges how much you do right.

Following the Celebration Guidelines will build good will between you, and make all your interactions more positive and easier.

Guidelines for Celebration

1. **Suggest a celebration.** *End each successful negotiation by saying": We did it! Now what do you want to do to celebrate?" By talking about what you need to create a feeling of celebration for both of you, you can quickly design your celebration to fit your accomplishment, and to have fun.*

2. **Create a celebration guide.** *Develop a list of the items or activities that really mean celebration to both of you: balloons, champagne or sparkling cider, friends or family around to help, using the best dishes and crystal, having a barbecue on paper plates, going out somewhere nice to eat, having a pizza delivered, buying tickets to a show, going to the movies, giving each other cards, making love, baking cookies, calling someone to share the good news, or just quietly congratulating each other on a job well done. Over a period of time together, you can develop a list of celebration items and activities that you can use as a resource each time you want to celebrate a successful negotiation.*

After Don found two friends to share an office suite with him and found reasonably priced, attractive space to share, he and Dale celebrated their decision three times. First, they got a sitter for Kendra and went out to dinner to their favorite restaurant. Then, they got together with the co-renters and had cake and coffee to celebrate and seal the deal. Finally, Don and his friends had an "office warming" party, at which Don made a speech acknowledging Dale for his help in coming up with the idea and helping to bring it all together.

Paul and Mary celebrated their decision to go to Lake Tahoe on an excursion deal by hugging and sending out for a pizza at the end of their negotiation, and then, at a special dinner during their vacation, they made a champagne toast to each other for being such smart negotiators. When they came home, they also bragged to their friends about how they had the best vacation of their lives, and that negotiation had helped them accomplish it.

Joe and Carol celebrated their decision to experiment with a housekeeper by eating take-out food on paper plates and throwing them away, so no one had to do any dishes.

John and Rose, whose decision was made after Stating Wants, celebrated by making love, and telling each other how much they appreciated their mutual caring and their communication.

You and your partner now have the basic tools you need for cocreating your ideal relationship. Because these skills, techniques, and attitudes are new and somewhat revolutionary compared to the way most people think relationships work, you will need to practice them. As you would with any new techniques, start with simple problems or purposely easy problems such as who takes out the trash or what the schedule for using the bathroom will be. Starting with simple problems gives you the greatest chance of success, and time to practice before you handle more difficult problems. Keep the Negotiation Tree handy for your first few negotiations. It will help you remember what step you are on, prevent you from skipping vital steps, and refer you back to sections in the book if you get "stuck" along the way. As your familiarity with cooperative negotiation increases, you will be able to handle more difficult problems. Your skills will gradually improve, as have most couples we work with, until you can handle your most emotional disagreements and complex problems without resorting to arguing or fighting.

Once you have sufficient practice, if a problem comes up that you cannot handle through Cooperative Problem Solving, you'll know that you need an independent outside expert, such as a marriage counselor, to help. The attempts you made at solving the problem cooperatively will save you time and money in counseling by clarifying where and how you are "stuck." Often, a problem that has been pre-discussed through the cooperative negotiation process can be solved in one or two counseling sessions, because the groundwork is already done.

Being skilled in cooperative negotiation makes it possible to work-out anything that troubles you, and even things that don't. With the changes you can make using these techniques, your way of being together will begin to take on a degree of comfort that feels great to both of you: your relationship will be satisfying, sustainable, and you will be on your way to Being a Couple and Still Being Free. The final chapter will show you how, once the day-to-day problems are solved, you can use Cooperative Problem Solving to shape and create a truly sustainable, cooperative partnership that is tailor made to your individual personalities and meets both of your needs to a degree you may not have dreamed possible.

## Chapter 7

# Feeling Free
Within Your
Partnership

Once you have mastered Cooperative Problem Solving through the use of the Negotiation Tree, you have a proven method you can use together to solve problems, resolve disputes, end conflicts: with the result that you both feel positive about yourselves, each other, and your ability to resolve difficult issues together.

What's more important, you now know that it is possible (and you have a method) for both of you to get what you want all the time, every time. These unlimited possibilities create a sense of freedom within your partnership, room for both of you to be fully who you are.

Most Common Issues for Cooperative Problem Solving

If you are like most couples, you will find yourselves experiencing the greatest number of problems—and therefore using Cooperative Problem Solving most often—about the following issues:

* *Romance*: The attractive, dramatic, and idealized relationships we see in movies and television (known as *romance*) combined with the excitement of the courtship phase of your relationship can create unrealistic expectations that lead to disillusionment and a sense of failure.

* *Lovemaking*: In a society where sexuality is both suppressed and exaggerated, and where the models presented in fiction are almost always based on the excitement of first love, couples often have no idea how sexuality works in long-term, committed relationships, or how to keep their sexual excitement alive.

* *Personality Quirks*: Each of us has individual behaviors and needs that don't conform to the preconceptions and expectations of our partners; and these can produce major struggles when we do not know how to effectively resolve and solve conflicts.

* *Good Times and Bad Times*: The natural ups and downs of life (illness, financial stress or windfall, career problems, promotions or changes, loss of a loved one, birth of a baby, parenting struggles, retirement, aging) have a strong impact on your relationship. Couples who do not know how to handle the down times often do not know how to handle the good times either.

* *Transitions*: Moving gracefully through the days and years, from work to play, and from one stage of life to another, is not always easy. Often when we are struggling with these transitions, we seem to find ourselves in incompatible modes, which lead to conflict and disagreement.

* *Forgiveness*: No two people can spend extended time together without making mistakes, hurting feelings, or making each other angry. If we do not know how to set these feelings aside and forgive ourselves as well as our partner, this anger festers and grows until it smothers the fires of love that brought us together and ends the relationship.

* *Challenges*: Many of us have old, unresolved pain from childhood events or "baggage" from past relationships. These unhealed emotional wounds can cause us to overreact to normal relationship problems and life challenges with overwhelmingly negative feelings and responses and make the problem seem unsolvable, causing serious relationship damage.

* *Unrealistic Limitations*: Couples are just as apt to be unrealistic in believing what they *cannot* do as they are in expecting themselves to do too much. When you believe you can't accomplish what you want to, you may not try at all or you'll give up too quickly and never get what you really want.

All of these barriers to freedom in your partnership can be overcome using the skills of Cooperative Problem Solving. As a couple, you build a sense of freedom by honoring each other's personalities, emotional needs, circumstances (such as family situations, financial realities, career demands, and the needs of children), individual quirks, foibles, faults, and problems. The steps of the Negotiation Tree guarantee that you have methods of confronting and overcoming all these factors when your work together to solve the related problems.

Romance

When couples live together for an extended period of time, the initial excitement and newness eventually wears off, and the heightened energy and excitement of being together (what we call romance) lessens because you get into a familiar daily routine. For example, when you lived separately and dated each other, every moment spent together was special, and it was easy to feel romantic. From the moment you begin to live together, such romantic moments are no longer automatic. Instead, much of your time together is spent on more mundane things: doing laundry, washing dishes, paying bills, or going to work. As soon as the initial newness of living together (often called the "newlywed" phase) wears off, such everyday things cease to feel exciting and romantic, and you may find yourself feeling worried that your partner no longer cares as much or is as excited to be with you.

Writing in *Men Are Just Desserts* (Warner Books, 1983), Psychologist Dr. Sonja Friedman maintains that this change is good: "Romance is a lovely diversion for a weekend, a honeymoon, a Thursday afternoon tryst, or as a momentary expression of affection on a special occasion, *but it's not a way of life*. While romance has a lot of fantasy going for it, love is grounded in reality...love requires real people who can be there to support each other through disheartening periods—grief, upsets, financial setbacks—and to share the joy from triumphs great and small."

Viewed this way, romance becomes a very useful tool you can use in conjunction with Cooperative Problem Solving to renew the energy in your relationship, whenever you feel the need. By using the Negotiation Tree (especially the State Wants and Explore Options and Decide sections) to solve the problem of lack of romance or excitement between you, you can create events and rituals that celebrate your love, affection, and desire for each other, which will remind and reassure each of you that you are special to the other.

To reenergize the romance in your relationship, you can:

* Arrange a date, a present, a surprise, a joke, or a hug when your emotional connection needs reinforcement.
* Meet at a singles bar, pretending to pick each other up, and winding up the evening at a motel.
* Act out fantasies, such as: photographer and model, movie star couple, nurse and doctor, stripper and audience member.
* Take a special vacation to a romantic spot together.
* Set aside one evening a week for a "date" and do what you used to do when you were courting.
* Spend a weekend morning having breakfast in bed.
* Send a card, a plant, flowers, cologne, or other present by messenger or leave them as a surprise on a day that's not normally a gift-giving occasion.
* Take a class together in something new and fun (mountain climbing, dancing, skiing, acting, roller-skating, pottery making, painting, stained glass, sailing, swimming, cooking) or get involved in your church, the community, or politics to create new experiences together.

The possibilities are endless, and these romantic "booster shots" to your relationship can keep it from becoming dull or routine. Use Cooperative

Problem Solving to develop the romantic ideas that will satisfy both of you because what feels romantic and loving to you may or not be similarly effective for your partner, and vice versa. The most helpful exercises you can use for developing new ideas are: Clarifying Your Wants (page 181), The Abundance Worksheet (page 208), Guidelines for Doing Research (page 212), and Guidelines for Celebration (page 225).

Lovemaking

Couples who have been together for a while find that their lovemaking changes and is different than it was when they were first dating, when their passion grew out of the excitement of the new and unknown. "As your affectionate love for your partner deepens, sex may lose some of its raw passion, explain Muriel Arund and Samuel Pauker in *The First Year of Marriage* (Warner Books, 1987). "At the same time...there are many benefits to a more emotionally intimate kind of sexual connection."

When you use Cooperative Problem Solving to meet both your needs as your relationship deepens, you will allow your lovemaking to change and grow as your partnership does, rather than holding to rigid expectations or getting stuck in repetitive patterns.

By using the Negotiation Tree you can create solutions for lovemaking under all sorts of conditions:

* *Quickies* sex (in a rush).
* *Sneaky sex* (getting around kids, in-laws, nosy neighbors).
* *Romantic sex* (for special occasions).
* *Newlywed sex* (the way you used to do it).
* *Make-up sex* (after a disagreement is solved).
* *Comforting sex* (when one of you is sad or stressed).
* *Relaxing sex* (slow, lazy, no pressure).
* *Reassuring sex* (affection and intimacy intended to reassure a partner who is temporarily insecure, or for reaffirming your mutual interest).
* *Fantasy sex* (playacting, role playing, dressing up).

The possible varieties of sexual attitudes, environments, energies, and activities are truly endless. A significant part of passion is the exploration of the unknown and, even when you've been together for many years, there can *still* be an unknown to explore if you approach each other as interesting, growing, and changing people and work together to meet your changing needs. The new solutions you create can keep your excitement and passion alive for a lifetime. Cooperative Problem Solving will help keep you from getting stuck in any one pattern, and allow yourselves an exciting variety of sexual expression. Cooperation creates an attitude of openness to what is happening right now, and responsiveness to each other and the moment, that is reminiscent of the way you approached lovemaking when you were new to each other.

Personality Quirks

Because we are all different from one another, with different backgrounds, experience, and early training, each of us has small quirks, personality traits or habits that must be accommodated, in one way or another, if we wish to have a sustainable relationship. These quirks (a laugh that grates on your nerves, differences in messiness or neatness, irritating jokes or stories, incompatible work schedules, and different ideas about TV programs or music, housekeeping, your partner's nail biting or smoking, what and when to feed the dog, how politely to speak to your children, or how warm the room should be) when endured for months and years, can feel like sufficient reason to get a divorce, or even commit mayhem. Many of these things may seem "silly" and so insignificant that you feel embarrassed to be so unhappy about them, but if you and your partner can't negotiate and resolve your frustration, small irritations can create enough resentment over time to become serious problems.

Guidelines: Dealing With Your Partner's Personality Quirks

When such small irritations happen, there are four things you can do.

1. Sometimes, your partner's quirks, such as being messy, picking at teeth, not putting lids back on jars tightly, watching too much TV, or singing off key, are small enough to be easily dismissed by deciding the "whole package" of your partner more than makes up for the little annoying habits. If you can do this without re-sentment, your partner's quirks will cease to be a problem, al-though occasionally you may need to remind yourself of the benefits of being together.

2. You can also voluntarily modify your own behavior (go to the bathroom to pick teeth, screw the lids on tight) to reduce the annoyance to your partner.

3. You can minimize (by leaving the room, or distracting yourself with a project) the impact of your partner's habits on yourself.

4. If the above three steps don't work, and you feel irritated and resentful about a quirk or habit, you and your partner can use the Negotiation Tree to discuss the problem objectively, without blame or defensiveness, to create solutions that satisfy both of you.

By using these guidelines, over time, you can create new ways to be partners for a lifetime without getting on each other's nerves; and create new options for dealing with the irritations when they arise.

Good Times, Bad Times

Although we all know that relationships go through good times and bad times, and that as partners, we'll probably face fights, tragedies, be-trayal, and struggle in a lifetime of living together, most people in new relationships (especially those who are in first-time relationships), want very much to believe that they will live "happily ever after." Hence, they avoid facing the harder facts: What happens if you lose your job? How are we going to handle it if we have money difficulties? What if one of us gets very sick? What if you have a lot more success at your career than I do at mine? What if we get more successful than we ever dreamed? Thus, when life is either very good or very difficult, couples often don't feel prepared to handle it.

In a lifetime of living together, you and your partner need to be able to handle many ups and downs:

* Problems to solve and victories to celebrate.
* Moments of excitement and moments of peace.

* Times of boredom and times of stressful activity.
* Fights and harmonious times.
* Tragedies and blessed events.
* Peaks of tremendous love and caring for each other.
* Valleys of distance and irritation.

Knowing how to use Cooperative Problem Solving means you can meet all these ups and downs as a team, work together to solve the problems, and celebrate your successes. Each experience that demonstrates you are a team who can remain calm in times of crisis, think problems through carefully, solve them in a way that satisfies both of you, and enjoy your successes to the fullest will strengthen your bond of trust and partnership, and cause you to feel more free in your partnership.

Transitions

As you grow older and gain more experience, your attitudes, expectations, and preferences change. Because your relationship is a reflection of the attitudes and experience of both of you, it must change as you do in order to sustain a mutual sense of freedom. These continuous changes, whether caused by circumstances (a new job means you must move to a new city), personal growth (you become more self-assured, and want to make some new friends or develop a talent), or an unexpected event (your spouse gets a serious illness) always create some turmoil and confusion.

When a couples' familiar way of doing things begins to change, they often begin to struggle, compete, or fight because one or both partners become insecure or frightened. However, when you know Cooperative Problem Solving, these transitions can become just a series of problems you must solve.

When John and Rose made the transition to John's retirement, they faced many new problems:

* How their finances would change on John's fixed retirement income.

* What John would do to keep active and involved now that he had a lot of unstructured time, and felt useless and lost.

* Whether to stay in their large house (designed for raising children) or sell it and move to a condominium.
* What limits to set on babysitting for their grandchildren.
* How Rose's new career would be affected by John's
retirement.
* How much traveling they would do together, where, and
in what way.

By solving each of these problems individually, rather than letting
themselves see the whole thing as one big retirement problem, John and
Rose were able to work out a balance between her career and his retirement that allowed them both to feel active and useful while still allowing them to enjoy leisure time and traveling.

You and your relationship will continue to grow and change, and
you won't always progress neatly from one stage to the next, or find an
arrangement that is permanently satisfying. Each of you can even be at
different stages at the same time! But, if you use the Negotiation Tree to
help you work out the confusion of new ways of doing things, and work
together to bridge the differences when they come up, you'll soon learn
to see each transition as an exciting new adventure or challenge instead of
a frightening change.

Forgiveness

In a lifetime of living together, we are bound to hurt each other's
feelings, betray trust, or let each other down from time to time, usually
without intending to. Some emotional hurts, such as when harsh words
are spoken in anger and frustration, or when an illicit affair occurs
during a relationship crisis, will only be resolved through healing and
forgiveness.

Cooperative Problem Solving helps us forgive because once we find
a solution to the problem that originally caused the hurt, teamwork makes
it much easier to "let go" of the hurt feelings and get back on good terms
with each other.

If you find you are holding hurt, anger, or resentment toward your
partner, use the Problem Inventory Exercise in Chapter 2 (page 61-65)

until you understand clearly enough to communicate the problem that needs to be resolved. Then proceed to solve whatever you feel hurt or angry about as if it were any other problem. You'll find that once you find a mutually satisfactory solution, forgiving your partner (and yourself) is made easier by the reassuring knowledge that the problem won't be repeated.

Challenges

Every relationship carries challenges to heal and grow. Because you and your partner are so intimately involved, your relationship is automatically an environment where old hurts and wounds from the past will arise. In fact, we often challenge each other in the very areas where we are wounded and most need to heal. It is so common for couples with corresponding unfinished issues to get together (a woman with an alcoholic father falls for a heavy drinker, a man whose mother was absent or distant is attracted to women who are similarly unavailable). When that happens, intimate, committed relationships often become arenas for facilitating healing and growth. If painful events happened in your childhood, such as physical or verbal abuse, incest, rape, the loss or death of a parent or sibling, or a severe injury or illness, a relatively mild incident could cause you to unexpectedly relive the pain of your early trauma. Partners who have had very painful past relationships (battering, cheating, lying, being left without warning, or severe financial damage, for example) can also carry unhealed psychological wounds that may cause them to overreact in a current relationship. No matter how loving you are, as partners you can unintentionally recreate old painful scenes from childhood or previous relationships. These become challenges you must overcome if you don't want to repeat destructive patterns from old relationships. The following guidelines will help you.

If you or your partner is overreacting to the problems because of old, unresolved hurt and trauma from childhood or a past relationship, you will see one or more of the following indicators:

1. You can't or won't discuss a particular topic, such as a gambling problem, a difficult in-law, sexual dissatisfaction, or disciplining the children.

2. A problem such as a partner's unreliability or lateness, a struggle over money, or jealousy, seems unsolvable or repeats.

3. You argue about different topics, but all of your arguments sound, feel and end the same. For example, you both yell until one of you storms out, or you don't speak for three days.

4. You can't negotiate about a particular topic, because you end up arguing.

5. One of you makes accusations including the words "you always" or "you never," indicating stored frustration, resentment, and anger about something the other does or doesn't do.

6. You feel highly critical, hopeless, angry or resentful about your partner's traits, like laziness, perfectionism, or lateness, or you become obsessed with making your partner see his or her "problem" and change it.

If any of the above indicators apply to your situation, you are probably facing a challenge in your relationship, and whenever you feel it is threatening to disrupt or destroy your partnership, you can use the following steps to overcome it.

Guidelines: Overcoming Challenges

1. Don't panic. *As painful and overwhelming as they may seem, challenges are common in relationships and can be overcome with Cooperative Problem Solving. Do your best to stay calm and use your Active Listening and Attentive Speaking skills to find out as much as you can about what the problem is, then follow the Negotiation Tree as you would with any problem. If you can't stay calm enough, go to Step 5.*

2. Develop temporary solutions. *Using the Guidelines for Doing Research (page 212) to develop temporary solutions (such as agreeing to call a time-out when issues get too heated) while you work separately using the Setting Aside Held Hurt and Anger Exercise (page 165) or, if necessary, a therapist in order to resolve the trauma or wounds from the past that are evoked by situations in your relationship.*

3. Be as supportive as you can. *If your partner is working on a challenging issue, do your best to be emotionally positive and encouraging. Reassure each other that you won't go away or avoid the issue. If the issue creates problems so difficult (violent outbursts, alcohol or drug addiction, severe sexual problems, emotional breakdowns) that you have to separate to protect yourself, you can still agree you'd be willing to resume your relationship once the problem is handled.*

4. Get outside support. *Select friends who can support both of you emotionally while you overcome the challenge, and don't hesitate to let them know when you need help. Having someone who cares, and who can listen and support without interfering, will relieve some stress and help you stay calm so you can use your Cooperative Problem Solving skills.*

5. Get professional help. *If you have used the above four steps and Cooperative Problem Solving and the problem still seems overwhelming, especially if one or both of you has a history of abuse, alcohol problems, rape or incest, get professional help. A therapist is an expert in just such issues, and can give you the objective, supportive feedback you need.*

Understanding the signs that indicate challenges, knowing that they exist to varying degrees in most relationships, learning to take care of yourself, recognizing that challenges present an opportunity to heal and grow, and knowing when to get help will increase your ability to overcome challenges and keep them from permanently damaging your partnership.

Challenges are another form of crisis that, when overcome through working together, strengthens your bond of confidence and trust in each other and in your partnership.

Unrealistic Limitations

Most couples that are not satisfied in their relationships have given in to unrealistic limitations. They are limited by false beliefs, *"shoulds,"* others' expectations, or their own lack of experience.

Because Cooperative Problem Solving is designed to help you develop new, previously unrealized ideas and solutions for problems, it is the perfect way to overcome unrealistic limitations. The Free Couple Relationship is based on the belief that both of you can get exactly what you want, all the time, with a profound respect for your individuality; and on working together lovingly to negotiate a relationship that suits you and your partner, whether you are traditional, modern, or radically different. Free Couple Relationships are not founded on the *form* of the relationship, but the *content:* the emotional satisfaction and practical functionality of a relationship that suits the people within it. A Free Couple knows they are a supportive and connected team.

Within a Free Couple Relationship, you can do *anything you both agree on.* You can live apart, but have a committed relationship, you can have two careers and still raise children, you can be a happy family with no children, you can switch traditional gender roles (for example, the man can stay home and raise children, the woman can earn all the money), you can be single parents who bring children together to form successful step families, you can live together and be celibate, monogamous, or have a sexually open relationship, you can own your own business and work together and maintain your loving relationship.

The whole point of having a mutual, cooperative partnership is to be able to do *what works for you.* The cooperative negotiation and communication skills you have learned here can help you work out any relationship you wish, provided both you and your partner are happy with the results. To overcome unnecessary limitations, use the Clarifying Wants Exercise in Chapter 5 and the Abundance Worksheet and the Brainstorming Exercises in Chapter 6 to help you design the relationship you want, and then use Cooperative Problem Solving to work out how to do it.

As you begin to eliminate these sources of struggle from the relationship, you will know you are on the way to becoming free, because you will experience the rewards:

* You feel supported by each other.
* You always have help and companionship in the hard places.
* You are aware of many advantages and reasons you are together.

* You have goals to work toward, and mutual successes to celebrate.
* When either of you experience difficulties or a failure, your partner knows how to offer solace and reassurance.
* You feel empowered because two people, pulling together, have more power than individuals working separately.
* You have the strength of commitment that comes from knowing that you and your partner are in the best relationship possible for each of you.
* You have the freedom to let your partnership take any form you and your partner want to give it.
* And best of all, your way of being together and your personal wants and needs are flexible enough to change over time as you as individuals change and grow.

Cooperative Problem Solving is a basic tool that you and your partner can use to renegotiate and modify your relationship to suit your individual changing circumstances as your experience of life changes your attitude and priorities.

By renegotiating each new situation as a Free Couple, you can create a relationship that changes and grows with you, rather than stagnating and beginning to confine one or both of you.

Ultimately, you will find that you have negotiated your way to a relationship that is unique. It does not look like anyone else's, and is custom-made to the specifications of you and your partner, who are as unique as your relationship.

As you grow together in this process you may find yourself willing to accept and try new ways of being together that would never have occurred to you before learning to brainstorm to find new solutions that satisfy both your wants.

John and Rose had adapted to the traditional relationship model their parents had felt comfortable with: John went to work and earned the money, and Rose took care of the house and the children. This worked fine for them until the children grew up. Then, suddenly, their old relationship focus changed, and Rose felt lost, unneeded, and dissatisfied. But, in following the steps of the Negotiation Tree, Rose and John explored the problem, uncovered "shoulds" and rules that were limiting them both, decided to try something different, and agreed that Rose would go to school. Her education led to her forming a new career as John approached retirement, and their new style of relationship, which ultimately was more enjoyable for both of them, was completely unlike any other relationship they knew.

For Fred and Naomi it was a two-step process: First they had to accept that they both had differing levels of sexual energy, and then they both had to accept the startling idea that it was all right for Fred to give himself pleasure at times when Naomi simply was not interested. Before using the Negotiation Tree, neither of them would have considered such an alternative.

Don and Dale found that, as job and financial circumstances changed, they needed more room and separate office space for Don's business, which meant their financial arrangement had to change. They kept using Cooperative Problem Solving over the years as Don's business grew, until his company filled an entire office building, and supported them both in style.

As these couples did, you will create a relationship that suits both the realities of your life and your individual needs and differences through learning and following the steps of Cooperative Problem Solving.

Goal-setting Enhances Partnership

Partners sometimes hesitate to discuss their hopes and dreams because they are afraid that their differences are basically incompatible, and therefore insurmountable, and sharing a vision of the future seems futile. However, when you have mastered Cooperative Problem Solving, you can resolve your differences as partners working together, and you'll discover accommodating divergent goals, overcoming the barriers to freedom in your relationship, and creating unique solutions to satisfy your wants deepens your bond and commitment and adds zest to your partnership.

Free Couples create a shared sense of purpose by setting relationship goals. When you have a clear vision of your personal and relationship goals (if we save money we can have our own business), all your mutual decisions can be made with your overall goals in mind (we'll choose a less expensive vacation, to save money). By working together to discover your mutual goals, you will gain a deeper understanding of your own as well as your partner's hopes and dreams, and the process of setting those goals together will help you know each other better. The love and mutual support you demonstrate to each other when you use your Cooperative Problem Solving skills over the years (caring about each other's wants, listening and understanding each other, working together to make sure both your wants are satisfied, making agreements you can keep, celebrating together), becomes your partnership foundation, free from the restrictions that lead to anger, resentment, and hurt. Love and mutual support reassure you in difficult times and make your joyful times more satisfying.

As a Free Couple, you can set many goals:

* *Emotional goals* (to make time together more fun and loving, or to share feelings more often).
* *Financial goals* (to save to buy a house).
* *Time goals* (to have more time alone together).
* *Health goals* (to go to the gym together three times a week, to eat a more low-fat diet).
* *Sexual goals* (to take a class in tantric yoga, to make time for sex at least twice a week, to experiment with a vibrator).
* *Career goals* (to put one of you through school, to start a business together).
* *Social goals* (to make some new friends, to help the homeless).
* *Recreational goals* (to go on vacation, to relax more on weekends).

In short, whenever you have wishes you have not yet created in your relationship, you can set goals to make your wishes come true by using the following guidelines.

Guidelines: Setting Partnership Goals

To set Free Couple goals, begin by using the Clarifying Your Wants Exercise (page 181) until your wishes are clear and easy to communicate. If your wants are different, use Cooperative Problem Solving to find a workable, mutually satisfying purpose you wish to accomplish. Then follow these steps:

1. Set your intention. *Once you know what you want, you need to agree to go for it. The combination of wanting something and being determined to accomplish it give you the direction and energy to act on your own behalf. The* confirm your decision *step of Cooperative Problem Solving (Chapter 6) will help you make sure your intention is mutual.*

2. Break your purpose down *into small steps that feel possible to work on, and list them. For example, if your wish was to attend college together, you could break that down into steps such as (1) go to the library and look up colleges to find three possibilities; (2) apply to all of them; (3) apply for student loans; and (4) enroll in school.*

3. Decide who will do which steps. *If it is not immediately obvious, use Cooperative Problem Solving to decide who does which steps. In the process of negotiating, you may find that the experience and expertise you gain as you work together will change either the steps or your stated purpose a bit, as it does in any experiment. Those changes are part of the learning process of setting goals and carrying them out.*

4. Do something. *Obviously, you won't achieve your goal if you never get around to doing anything. Breaking your goal down into small steps should help you feel less overwhelmed and more motivated. However, if you find that you are not doing what you agreed to, go back to Guideline 2 and break the goal into smaller, easier steps or use your Active Listening and Attentive Speaking skills (pages 98, 102) to find out what is in the way.*

5. Celebrate what you've accomplished. *Use the Guidelines for Celebration (page 225) to celebrate every step you complete, to keep your enthusiasm high and create motivation.*

By setting your intention, creating small steps, and completing and celebrating each step of your plan as you go along, you'll find that you have changed your relationship in the desirable ways you want, and that even the work of creating change has been fun. After a few goal-setting successes, you'll find that your sense of commitment and confidence in your partnership grows stronger. Your Free Couple Relationship will meet your needs so well and will be so comfortable and suitable for both of you that there will be no sense of limitation or restriction. In this way, creating a free partnership is a by-product of seeking your mutual satisfaction through Cooperative Problem Solving.

Your relationship becomes free because it contains none of the problems that might cause you to feel you are losing your individual identity or that you're in bondage. Rather than fight, you work together; rather than feeling deprived, you both feel fulfilled; rather than being frustrated, you find solutions; rather than being defeated, you experience success; rather than restricting yourselves, you are each free to be yourself.

Cooperation and negotiation are powerful tools because they are completely flexible and applicable to almost any possible relationship situation. Although it may take some practice to feel comfortable with these new tools, by learning to use them well, you'll be maximizing your chances for success in your relationship. As an added bonus, you'll increase the pleasure and satisfaction in your partnership and in your lives together.

 # Bibliography

Arund, Muriel and Samuel Parker. *The First Year of Marriage.* New York: Warner Books, 1987.

Bradshaw, John. *Healing the Shame That Binds You.* Deerfield Beach: Health Communications, 1988.

Friedman, Sonya. *Men Are Just Desserts.* New York: Warner Books, 1983.

Gordon, Dr. Tom. *Parent Effectiveness Training*

Hay, Louise. *You Can Heal Your Life.* Santa Monica, Calif.: Hay House, 1984.

Hayes, Jody. *Smart Love.* Los Angeles: J. P. Tarcher, 1989.

Holladay, Frosty. "Love That Works," *In Context Magazine,* Summer 1985.

Johnson, Robert A. *We: Understanding the Psychology of Romantic Love.* New York: Harper and Row, 1983.

Kantrowitz, Barbara "Breaking the Divorce Cycle" *Newsweek,* January 13, 1992.

Leigh, Wendy. "Learning How to Love When Passion Dies" *New Woman Magazine,* April 1985.

Roberts, Denton. *Able and Equal: A Gentle Path to Peace.* Culver City, Calif.: Human Esteem Publishing, 1984.

Sellner, Judy and Jim Sellner. "Falling in Love for Keeps: the Six Stages of Love" *New Woman,* November 1985.

Index

About the Authors

Tina B. Tessina, Ph.D., LMFT, has 25 years of experience as a licensed marriage and family therapist. She is the author of 10 books including: *The Ten Smartest Decisions A Woman Can Make After Forty* (Renaissance, 2001) *The Unofficial Guide to Dating Again* (Hungry Mind, 1999) *The 10 Smartest Decisions A Woman Can Make Before 40* (HCI, 1998) *The Real Thirteenth Step: Discovering Confidence, Self-Reliance and Autonomy Beyond the Twelve Step Programs* (Tarcher, 1991; revised ed. Career Press, 2001), *Gay Relationships: How To Find Them, How To Improve Them, How To Make Them Last* (Tarcher, 1989 soft-cover 1990), *and Lovestyles: How To Celebrate Your Differences* (Newcastle, 1987). Her books have been published in 11 languages.

Dr. Tessina lectures and conducts workshops nationwide on all of her books, and has appeared on major television and radio shows, including *Donohue, The Oprah Winfrey Show, Geraldo*, and *Larry King Live*. She lives in Long Beach, California, with her husband, Richard Sharrard.

AUG 2 2 2002

To reach Dr. Tessina for questions, lectures, workshops, and individual and couple therapy:

Tina B. Tessina, Ph.D. LMFT
License MX 13629
P.O. Box 4883
Long Beach, CA 90804
562-438-8077
Web site: *www.tinatessina.com*
E-mail: tinatessina@compuserve.com

Riley K. Smith, M.A., is a Licensed Marriage and Family Therapist who has been helping couples and individuals create satisfying relationships since 1976. He supervises and teaches therapists in addition to his psychotherapy practice.

He lives in Los Angeles with his life partner, Rhoda Pregerson, who is also a psychotherapist.

Tina Tessina and Riley K. Smith also wrote: *True Partners: A Workbook for Developing Lasting Intimacy* (J.P. Tarcher, 1992) and *Equal Partners* (Hodder and Stoughton, London, 1994).